THE SACRED ANOINTING

BOOKS BY STEVEN BROOKS

Working With Angels

Standing on the Shoulders of Giants

AVAILABLE FROM DESTINY IMAGE PUBLISHERS

THE SACRED ANOINTING

The Power to Live Your Dream

STEVEN BROOKS

DESTINY IMAGE® PUBLISHERS, INC.

P.O. Box 310, Shippensburg, PA 17257-0310

"Speaking to the Purposes of God for This Generation and for the Generations to Come."

This book and all other Destiny Image, Revival Press, MercyPlace, Fresh Bread, Destiny Image Fiction, and Treasure House books are available at Christian bookstores and distributors worldwide.

For a U.S. bookstore nearest you, call 1-800-722-6774.

For more information on foreign distributors, call 717-532-3040.

Or reach us on the Internet: www.destinyimage.com.

ISBN 10: 0-7684-3204-9

ISBN 13: 978-0-7684-3204-6

For Worldwide Distribution, Printed in the U.S.A.

2 3 4 5 6 7 8 9 10 11 / 14 13 12 11 10

Table of Contents

Foreword

The Sacred Anointing is a book that will kindle a desire within you to breathe in the stimulating fragrances of Heaven. I believe Steven has brought forth a valuable work that will enable hearts to draw near to the Lord. In my fifty-plus years of ministry, I have seen and experienced the costly price of the anointing, as well as the ability of the anointing to accomplish miracles, which truly only God can perform.

At this present time in which many place an emphasis on polished human ability, it is a blessing to read a book that issues a bold challenge for the Church to aim for the glorious results that can be attained only when we operate in the anointing. There is no substitute for the moving of the Spirit.

Steven is one who has developed a keen sensitivity to flowing in the Spirit.

Steven demonstrates the willingness to pay the price for the sacred anointing, which originates out of a life devoted to prayer and waiting on the Lord, along with the diligent study of the Word. As you read this book, you will see the source of his strength, with clear insight as to why he is known for having a "*miracle ministry.*"

You too, can move into a greater realm of the "*miraculous*" through the truths contained within this book. Expect to receive an impartation into your spiritual life experience, along with a deep desire to become a pure vessel that the Lord might flow His mighty Spirit through. The practical stories and prophetic insight by Steven reveal how to increase God's anointing upon your life.

Steven operates from the position in which he recognizes the need for a heavenly empowerment to be "*upon*" him. Through this, he has learned many "*secrets of the anointing*" that will be applicable to you as well. You will be inspired to pray, and also, to receive a quickening to lay aside every weight that could hinder you from increasing in your spiritual growth and development.

Now is the time for *you* to experience God's sacred anointing in a fresh and new way, as you prayerfully read this anointed book.

Dr. Wade Taylor
Washington, D.C.
Internationally recognized author and Bible teacher

Preface

This book was written in response to a divinely granted visitation I received from the Lord Jesus in the summer of 2008, which occurred while ministering in Berlin, Germany. I had been fasting with only one small meal a day, and was on my twenty-second day of fasting and seeking God with much prayer. The fasting combined with an international travel schedule had left me physically tired, but until the twenty-second day of my fast I never suffered from being hungry. The Lord had supernaturally lifted my appetite for 21 days. On the twenty-second day of the fast, my appetite came back in full force. Suddenly, I noticed all the bratwurst, apple strudel, and other German delights that were all around me. The grace for fasting had lifted.

Despite the great hunger, I was determined to continue to fast because of a certain breakthrough I was seeking from the Lord. That Saturday I was in prayer most of the day; I was preparing for the evening service in which I was to minister. My wife and other guests had left the apartment we were staying in and had gone into town for the day. My daughter was the only other one in the apartment, and she was happily occupied reading and relaxing. This allowed me to seek the Lord with undistracted attention.

I found the quietest place in the apartment, which was a very small laundry room overlooking the courtyard. This little room was only large enough to hold a washer/dryer unit and a shelf to put the laundry soap on. It wasn't designed for a person to be in. The door to this room was only four feet tall! You had to bend low to enter in, and there was no room to even turn around. But it was quiet and the perfect place for prayer. There was even a small window that allowed sunlight to come in. I was in prayer most of the day, but the strong hunger for food was proving to be a distraction. I continued in prayer until the late afternoon, when suddenly the Lord Jesus appeared before me in a vision in that small laundry room!

He stood about five feet in front of me. The first thing Jesus said to me was, "I would like for you to start eating again." He said this with kindness, but also with strength to let me know that my time of fasting was complete. This certainly was evident since there was no longer any grace from the Holy Spirit to fast. He continued by saying, "I've come to talk with you about your third book. In this book you are to do less teaching and more prophetic writing." (You will notice that in my two former books, *Working With Angels* and *Standing on the Shoulders of Giants,* I endeavor to explain certain spiritual experiences in order to show the biblical foundation for such events.)

Jesus knew I would be hesitant to share certain stories without trying to explain from the Scriptures that miraculous visitations and other experiences are valid today. Often when you speak about the supernatural, people (especially church people) think you are strange. I know this all too well from experience. But the Lord read my thoughts and replied, "My people are ready now. Do not hold back from that which I have allowed you to experience, or the things which I will be revealing to you." He went on to share with me that I would be "caught up" in the realm of the Spirit as well as to Heaven at times in order to receive revelation and insight that I was to share in this book. By God's grace I've endeavored to obey the Lord's instructions that came on that special day. I also enjoyed my remaining time in Germany by regaining the weight that I lost from fasting. When it was time to fly home, the local bakeries and deli shops were sad to see me leave!

The Lord's visit to me was also a clear confirmation of a prophetic word that I received two months earlier from a dear friend who is an internationally known prophet. When Jesus spoke with me, He shared some of the same things that this seasoned prophet said through his prophetic utterance to me. The Lord, however, gave me much more detail as He personally conversed with me. The Lord will always confirm and bring to pass a true prophetic word. The gift of prophecy is still alive in the Church today.

Writing this book proved to be a deeply moving experience. Often the fragrances of the Lord would gently but clearly sweep over me as I would write late into the night. In this book I share in detail about the spiritual meaning of these fragrances, and I believe that as you meditate on these Scriptures, you will experience this grace as well.

We have much to look forward to as the Lord is now ready to release His glory through the Church in unprecedented measures. It truly is an honor to be a part of God's plan for the great end-time harvest. Prepare your heart to move in the sacred anointing like never before!

Double Blessings,
Steven Brooks

CHAPTER ONE

The Sacred Anointing

The anointing of the Spirit of God is one of the most priceless attributes one can ever steward. It's far more valuable than gold or the most precious jewels. The anointing surpasses earthly value, for it is a divine substance that flows directly from God Himself. The anointing may be displayed through various manifestations of the Spirit, but all such manifestations will glorify Jesus and bring honor unto His holy name.

The anointing of God has the ability to accomplish what man can never do. When the situation is hopeless and there is no natural means of help, then God truly can receive all the glory when He brings forth His deliverance. Recently I was ministering in South India in a healing crusade. The Spirit of God was resting upon me with a strong anointing for miracles. We had already seen notable miracles occur in the meetings, which were testified of before many witnesses. I always enjoy experiencing the power of God. The anointing is the burden-removing, yoke-destroying power of God. But the anointing is more than just power.

The character of Jesus is displayed through the miracles He performs. On the last night of the healing crusade, the faith of the congregation was so high that miracles were happening all over the place. The people left their seats and crowded to the front, pushing forward in a desperate act to receive healing from God while the anointing was in strong manifestation. Even with all the ushers it was difficult to control the crowd. The pastor said, "There are too many people, so we will run them by you in a line, and you just touch them when they go by."

The people began to stream by me like a flowing river of humanity. The line was moving quickly, but suddenly in the line I saw a young girl, about four or five years of age, coming toward me. Her mother was behind her, gently pushing her forward. When I saw this young girl, it seemed as if everything went into slow motion. What took place in the natural only lasted for about three seconds, but in the spirit realm it seemed timeless. As she stepped toward me, our eyes met. There was an instant connection. The young girl smiled at me with a sparkle in her eyes. She reminded me of my young daughter who was at home on the other side of the world. The pastor standing next to me spoke and said, "That girl is a deaf-mute."

The line was pushing the young girl forward so quickly that all I had time to do was reach out with my left hand as far as I could. Both of my hands were dripping with anointing oil because that evening I had been laying hands on the sick. I was able to reach out and quickly run my finger across her lips. She looked at me again and smiled with the anointing oil shimmering on her lips, and then vanished into the crowd of people as the line continued off in a different direction. The whole thing happened so quickly. I couldn't have touched those tiny lips of hers with such precision even if I had tried to do it on purpose. I'm not that coordinated. But that's what the anointing is. The anointing is slippery; it makes that which would be considered difficult or impossible to do seem to be done easily and smoothly.

It was about 30 minutes later when I had completed touching all those who came through the line. The pastor then wanted to take me to the back of the church where I could rest. As we walked toward the back, we came across that little girl and her mother. We found the young girl jumping around and making all kinds of noises. After I touched her lips in the prayer line, her ears had popped open and her tongue had been unloosed! Touched by the power of God, she was now able to clearly say, "Jesus, Jesus, Jesus!" From being a deaf-mute to hearing and speaking—that's what the anointing of God can do. To me, that's not just another miracle. The anointing is not only revealed as a demonstration of power, but as an expression of that which is sacred, holy, and precious. That special moment when the eyes of the young Indian girl caught mine and a divine connection was made is one example of many that I have experienced in which something from Heaven touches the ocean floor of the heart. Those are moments when time vanishes and unseen angels snap photos of what will decorate the walls of our future heavenly home. I have had miracles happen in my ministry that could be considered more powerful, but if we look with open hearts beyond just the physical miracle, we often see deeper truths that are hidden.

For instance, in that same healing crusade, I had ample opportunity to prove that there is no sickness or disease that the Lord Jesus cannot heal. The crusade started on a Saturday evening. Before the service began, some of the loyal and dedicated church members had gone into the local village and invited the sick to come. Many of the people they invited were Hindus. The believers told the Hindus that if they would come to the meeting, the man of God would pray for them and the Lord Jesus Christ would heal them. Well, a whole group of Hindus who had never been in a church service in their entire lives came to the meeting. They came sick and needing a miracle. The sicknesses they had were not something you could fix by giving them an aspirin. These were tough cases such as leprosy, open and infected running sores, demon possession, blindness, deafness, paralysis, and a host of other diseases that had no intention of leaving. The luxury of being able to go to a doctor was not an option for them. These precious people could never afford that. It was either receive a miracle or continue to live in pain, torment, and misery. This is where the rubber meets the road and the true Gospel is verified.

The pastor was very gracious to the new Hindu guests who came that night. He put them all on the front row and made them feel very welcome. I preached a good message, but I knew the whole time I was preaching that most of the Hindus weren't interested in my sermon. They were simply waiting for me to pray for them. They wanted proof, not talk, that what I was preaching was real. Today in our churches we have too much preaching and not enough demonstration. Ministers must be willing to move past their comfort level of just preaching and step out in faith to operate in the spiritual gifts. I love hearing good preaching, but we must also give the Holy Spirit opportunity to move.

As the anointing came upon me to minister to the sick, I quickly moved to close my message. The musicians took their places on their instruments to assist me, and I began to pray first for some of the church members who needed healing. As I did so, miracles began to happen. Pain began to leave, and diseases departed. The Hindus on the front row were watching intently, and when they saw the miracles, they got out of their seats and came forward without even being asked. They were hungry; they were desperate.

As I laid hands on the Hindus, God began to heal them! Paralysis began to leave; deaf ears began to pop open. God was responding to their faith. It's interesting when you operate in the Spirit because you become more sensitive to the anointing than you are to natural things. But even under the anointing your mind still works and is fully aware of what is going on. That evening before I began to pray for the sick I was aware of those in the meeting who I could see needed a miracle. As I mentioned earlier, those on the front row were in horrible condition. But, in the midst of those great needs there was one particular individual who, in my estimation, seemed in a far worse condition than them all.

Someone had brought a young woman into the meeting and laid her in someone's lap on the front row. She appeared to be in her early twenties. She was suffering from some type of abnormal paralysis and had very little control over her body. She also was unable to see anything even though her eyes were open. She appeared to be demon possessed, and she had a look in her eyes that suggested "nobody was home." As she lay in the lap of someone who was holding her, she looked like a sack of potatoes, just limp, lifeless, and pitiful. My heart grieved when I saw her, and in my natural mind I thought, "Whew! This one is worse than all of them!"

But as miracles began to happen, guess who ended up in the line in front of me? You guessed it—that young woman. I began to minister to her in the power of the Spirit. I'll be honest with you and say I prayed for her with as much intensity as I've ever released. I don't believe in half-hearted efforts. A deep and passionate prayer came out of my belly, and I took several minutes to continually keep my hands on her as I called out to a merciful God. The Lord had me cast out the devil that possessed her. I knew a miracle had happened. By the Spirit I also knew that a miracle healing anointing had flowed from God, through me, and into her body. When she was escorted away, it looked like not much had changed, but I knew God was going to get glory out of this.

We closed the meeting that night thankful for the miracles we saw. The next morning was Sunday morning, and the crowd had gone from 600 people on Saturday evening to about 2,000 that morning. The praise and worship was wonderful. The people were expecting God to move. He didn't disappoint. Just as the praise and worship session was ending, guess who came walking into the building in front of all those people? It was that young woman for whom I had prayed the night before! She came walking in with rays of light streaming out of her face! She walked like a royal dignitary with perfect posture and fluid, graceful strides. She was smiling, and her vision was perfect. The pastor about fell over! It shook the church to the core. The pastor grabbed her and immediately took her up on the stage for everyone to see. The people marveled as she walked back and forth on the stage, even up and down the stairs of the choir platform, with total ease. She testified of how God's healing power went into her body when I laid hands on her and prayed for her the night before. As she testified, rays of light were shining through her face. It was glorious. As you can imagine, the service that morning was a landslide. Miracles were happening with as much ease as drinking a glass of water. The pastor told me later that this young woman was a Muslim—it is very rare for a Muslim to come to a Christian church in that part of India. But she was touched and changed by God, and she has the same name as my stepdaughter Jennifer, who is very close to me.

I'm so glad I obeyed and positioned myself to receive the Lord's sacred anointing. When you have personally seen and experienced His glory, you are never the same. There is a place where church games no longer satisfy you. No longer are you content to settle with "a little dab will do ya." No, you want more. You want the biblical standard found in the Book of Acts and displayed throughout the Word of God. You hunger for real revival, genuine heavenly fire, and true spiritual gifts, things for which there is no substitute. For too long we have traded the glory of God for pampered seats and fancy, high-tech sanctuaries that thrill our senses but are void of the moving of God's Spirit. I'm all for comfortable, theatre-style seats and a state-of-the-art sound system, but I would rather meet in a laundromat if the Spirit of God were moving there, then in the most lavish meeting room where God's Spirit is stifled and suppressed.

Have we forgotten the Upper Room in Jerusalem where the Spirit of God fell in power? They didn't have stained glass windows or ceiling fans or padded carpet to comfortably kneel on. Despite their simplicity, God poured out His Spirit on the 120 souls who were present on the day of Pentecost. It shook all of Jerusalem and eventually flowed out to the nations of the world. The Church and the world have never been the same since. It's time the Church got back down on her knees and prayed as they did in the Upper Room. There will never be a substitute for fervent prayer. The Church has tried just about every other gimmick possible to reach the lost. By endeavoring to do so without prayer, we have drifted from the message of the cross and have replaced it with countless feel-good sermons. Whatever happened to sermons that convicted the hearer of sin? Yes, we need to be made to feel loved and assured; we need to be reminded that we are blessed. But we don't need to hear just those types of messages all the time.

Have we failed to remember how God moved at Azusa Street in an old renovated horse stable during the years of 1906–1910? Because the old building the saints met in used to be a stable for horses, cows, and sheep, the saints constantly had a problem with flies. Though they cleaned it to the best of their ability, the flies still showed up. You would be amazed by how little resistance it takes to keep some Christians from receiving their miracle. Some let the smallest hindrance hold them back from the blessings of God, such as a little headache or a fly. Those meetings were well before my time. If I was alive then, I would have gone to those meetings with a flyswatter—but I would've been there!

Even with a sawdust-covered, dirt floor and lack of proper ventilation, people came from around the world by the thousands to be in that wonderful move of God's Spirit. I've read the testimonies of when the glory of God would come into the meetings. Sometimes the "glory cloud" would rest about one foot or 18 inches above the ground. Because of this, many of the saints would lay on the ground to get into the cloud. As they lay on the ground in the cloud, they would breathe the atmosphere of Heaven. I don't blame them; I would do the same thing. A person who desperately needs a miracle often goes through the process of casting off the prideful garments of religious dignity in the course of being healed.

Why would Elisha give instructions for Naaman to wash in the Jordan River? Naaman was perplexed by such a directive that ran contrary to his position of high rank and elitist mentality. He was a wealthy military general. He was the king's closest advisor, and he was accustomed to wealth. He also had a temper and was full of pride and arrogance. But God's answer for Naaman and his leprous condition was for him to bathe seven times in the Jordan River. God sent Naaman on purpose to a river that was so muddy that after bathing in it you would have to rinse off somewhere else to get clean. Despite initial resistance, Naaman eventually obeyed and received his miracle. God longs to move upon our hearts as we humbly yield to His will.

It's amazing to me sometimes where and how God chooses to move. I was ministering once to the Nepalese people up in the Himalayan Mountain region. A dear minister friend invited me to be one of the main speakers at a youth conference of about 450 young people, from the ages of 15 to 29. It was cold, and the conditions were challenging, but I wouldn't trade anything for the honor of being where God chooses to display His glory. Most of the young people attending the meetings were not wealthy. Most were believers, but they knew very little about the Lord. They came from the surrounding areas, which have much poverty and very high crime rates. Drug usage, sexual immorality, and a host of other sins plagued many of them. As believers, they had accepted salvation, but there was still much bondage in their lives. As the meetings progressed over a period of five days, God began to break through to their hearts.

There was deep repentance that came forth from the young people. They would cry out to God to be filled with the Holy Spirit. There was also much sorrow over unrepentant sins. Several times in those meetings the Spirit of God fell in tremendous power. In one particular service, a golden rain fell on everyone in the meeting, and we were inside a building! You could look up with your face toward Heaven and literally feel golden drops of sunlight splashing on your face. It was outrageously delightful. All of us experienced it together. It was glorious to just stand in that heavenly rain; it was like standing beneath an outpouring of pure, sparkling, liquid light. There wasn't a person in the building who didn't have a glow on his or her face. We all felt like royalty, with a deep knowing that we are children of the King.

I know some who read this will think, *"That's great those things happen in other countries, but what about America?"* Honestly, I've seen God move in miracle power as strongly here in America as I've seen anywhere else in the world. This nation is primed for a great move of God's Spirit. Miracles are happening here all the time. Soon we are going to see professional sport stadiums packed full of people for revival meetings. We are going to see entire hospitals have all their patients healed. We are pushing toward an explosion of faith so powerful that it will generate miracles that cannot be hidden or explained away. Denominational barriers will disappear as the saints work together to capture the harvest. God is not going to let the devil outdo Him. Although the enemy has come in like a flood upon this nation with unprecedented filth and lewdness, the Spirit of God is going to raise a standard that cannot be overcome. God is not about to let a rogue, outlaw, fallen rebel angel (satan) outdo Him in manifestations of power.

Under the old covenant, God worked through the prophet Elijah, who called down fire. That's not the only time that has happened in history. Not too many years ago, there was a prophet of God who lived on an island southwest of India who called down fire from Heaven before hundreds of witnesses, and the fire fell! Displays of God's power are forthcoming. There will be prophets who walk boldly into cities of great pride and arrogance and announce impending destruction if there is not repentance. Jonah being sent to Nineveh was not a onetime event. In Jonah's day, Nineveh was the largest city in the world! What if that happened today in New York City, Dallas, or Los Angeles?

I have an announcement to make: "Bible days are here again." Many have read the stories in the Bible, but for many people that's all they are—just stories. But Jesus Christ is the same yesterday, today, and forever. The God of Elijah and Jonah is still the same God today. The devil has released such a deluge of evil that only the Spirit of God can turn the tide. I know the devil can do counterfeit miracles, but the devil is not going to be able to match what God is now releasing. When Aaron threw his rod down before Pharaoh, it turned into a snake. The magicians (warlocks) of Pharaoh duplicated the miracle, but Aaron's snake consumed the magicians' snakes (see Exod. 7:8-13). God will not be outdone.

God desires to release His precious anointing upon us and through us, but we must be open to His promptings and be willing to accommodate His Spirit. Once you have been touched with the sacred anointing, your view of what a successful meeting is takes on a different viewpoint. It's the anointed Word coupled with the Spirit's power that is able to free our souls from pride, spiritual lethargy, and religious boredom. It's time for the glory to fall. It's time for the oil of the Spirit to flow unhindered into the deepest chambers of our hearts, and thus outward to a hurting and dying world.

God wants to touch your heart and anoint you with fresh oil. He wants to develop sensitivity in your heart to be able to move with His Spirit at the slightest leading. It's miracles like the few I've mentioned that make it worthwhile to pay the price for the sacred anointing. The anointing is costly. The price to pay is not measured in monetary value, but rather in obedience to God and in a willingness to lay our whole lives before Him. God is a giver of good gifts. Obedience to

His Word and the leading of the Spirit are necessary requirements to advancing in the anointing. The Lord releases His
best to us as we choose to give Him our best in all that we
do. God greatly desires that His people be anointed. I believe
the anointing of God is coming upon your life in a fresh and
powerful way.

CHAPTER TWO

Discovering the Source of the Anointing

In the Old Testament the special oil used for the purpose of anointing was considered sacred. It wasn't poured on just anybody or anything. What does "to anoint" mean? According to biblical Hebrew, it means to "rub down and smear with oil."[1] We clearly see in the Bible that Jesus was anointed. Some people think that *Christ* is Jesus' last name. However, *Christ* is a title, which means, "The Anointed One." When did the anointing come upon Jesus? Was He born anointed, or was it something He received at a particular time? In the Gospel of Matthew, we see the moment when Jesus became anointed.

When He had been baptized, Jesus came up immediately from the water; and behold, the heavens were opened to Him, and He saw the Spirit of God descending like a dove and alighting upon Him (Matthew 3:16).

The Spirit of God came to rest upon Jesus when He came up out of the water. This is the exact moment that Jesus became anointed. After this experience, He was immediately sent by the Spirit of God into the wilderness to be tempted by the devil. He overcame the temptations of the enemy and then launched into His ministry.

And Jesus went about all Galilee, teaching in their synagogues, preaching the gospel of the kingdom, and healing all kinds of sickness and all kinds of disease among the people. Then His fame went throughout all Syria; and they brought to Him all sick people who were afflicted with various diseases and torments, and those who were demon-possessed, epileptics, and paralytics; and He healed them (Matthew 4:23-24).

Not one miracle of Jesus is recorded in the Bible until *after* He became anointed. We see that Jesus was anointed by the Spirit of God during His water baptism at the Jordan River. There is a time and place when the Spirit of God can place an anointing upon someone.

I clearly remember the day when the healing anointing came upon my life. Before this anointing came, I prayed for the sick, but I could only pray the prayer of faith because I had no special anointing to minister to the sick. Nevertheless, I saw many receive healing because faith in God's Word will work. For instance, I prayed for a man who was in great discomfort and had limited mobility because of a severe hernia that had been diagnosed by a medical doctor. I laid my hands on Him and asked God to heal his body. There was no tangible anointing present, simply a prayer based upon God's Word, which says,

> *And these signs will follow those who believe: In My Name...they will lay hands on the sick, and they will recover* (Mark 16:17-18b).

He left the meeting that day, and I did not see him again until three weeks later. The next time I saw him he was walking normally and had no pain in his body. I asked him about the hernia and he said after I prayed for him all the pain left. He then went back to the same doctor and was rechecked, and the doctor said there was nothing wrong with him. I then said to him, "Jesus healed you. You should praise God and testify of how Jesus healed you." He replied to me, "Well, I don't know. The doctor said he must have originally misdiagnosed me. He said he was certain there was a hernia there, but after reexamination there is nothing there except a little piece of fatty tissue." Jesus healed this man, and he didn't recognize his own miracle! Even before the healing anointing came, however, there were many times that people testified of having been healed when I prayed for them. That's because God's Word is true, and you don't have to have a special anointing to see results. All you need is faith in God's Word.

While the *prayer of faith* will heal the sick, we see in the four Gospels that Jesus ministered with a *healing anointing*. The anointing often produces instant miracles. The healing anointing works best on unbelievers. It will also work for any Christian as well, but as a believer matures in their walk with God there comes a point where God expects us to believe His Word, whether there is a tangible anointing present or not. If you receive an instant miracle of healing because of the anointing, you will praise God and be thankful. But if your miracle is not instant, and you have to pray, confess the promises of God's Word, and hold to the Word of God despite opposing symptoms, then when your healing comes there has also been a tremendous development of your faith that will continue to be very useful, even after the miracle.

In the summer of 2006 I held some meetings in Irving, Texas. After those meetings were complete, I had about ten days until my next ministry engagement. My older brother lived close to Irving, so I went to his house to relax for a few days. During this time, I began reading a book about John G. Lake. This was a large book of over 500 pages, and I wasn't originally planning on reading the whole book. I actually wanted to verify a certain statement that I thought Dr. Lake had made.

As you may know, Dr. Lake had a powerful apostolic ministry to the nation of South Africa in the early 1900s. After completing his ministry in Africa, he returned to the state of Washington, where he opened Lake's Divine Healing Institute in the city of Spokane. Some have claimed that his ministry so impacted the city that the United States government declared Spokane the healthiest city in the world![2] Glory to God! How would you like to have someone like that living in your hometown? If there's not someone like that, then why don't you be that person?

I started out reading the last hundred pages of the book. I never found the quotation I was looking for, so I decided to read the first hundred pages. It wasn't there, either. I kept reading, and before I knew it, I had read the whole book over a two-day period. I never found the quotation I was looking for, but I did find something else. Reading all the stories of healing miracles had done something to my faith. After hours of reading and meditating on those stories, it seemed easy to believe God for miracles. As I was pondering all that I had read over those two days, I was suddenly interrupted by screams from my daughter, as she ran into the room crying and frantically saying, "Daddy, Daddy, get them off of me!"

I looked at her and didn't notice anything wrong. I asked her what was wrong, and she said, "The fire ants were all over my legs." As she stood there, red welts began to break out all over her legs. She had been playing in the backyard with her cousin and unknowingly sat down in grass that was loaded with fire ants. She had managed to brush most of the ants off, but not without having been stung all over her legs. As I looked at her legs, I could suddenly visualize all the nights of sleep I was going to lose from having to deal with the pain and itching that she was sure to have to endure. Those red fire ants are infamous in Texas. A friend of mine was once stung by a bunch of them and suffered in misery for four months and had to have prescription antibiotics to deal with the effects.

As I looked at my daughter, the Spirit of God flashed within me. I gently took her by the hand and said, "Come with Daddy, I'm going to pray for you." I knew beyond a shadow of a doubt that God was going to heal her. We went to a side bathroom for privacy so that I could pray for her.

When I looked at her legs, I saw at least 30 red welts that were getting bigger by the moment. I placed my hands on her legs and with authority rebuked the poison and all symptoms of those ant stings. With God and my daughter as witnesses, I want you to know that all of those welts instantly disappeared! The redness, swelling, and itching were completely gone. My daughter has seen and personally experienced God's healing power many times. What appeared to be an unpleasant and painful situation turned into an opportunity for God to receive glory. On that day, the healing anointing came upon my life, and it has been there ever since. It was like receiving a new suit. I had to learn how to wear it, use it, and understand it. Since then, the anointing has gotten stronger, and I've learned how to accommodate the increase.

As I mentioned earlier, Jesus ministered with a healing anointing. There are different ways in which an individual can be anointed, but the healing anointing is a very sacred anointing. In this book I want to give special attention to the healing anointing because this anointing is coming upon the Body of Christ in increased measure and in a more widespread distribution.

> How God **anointed** Jesus of Nazareth with the **Holy Spirit** and with **power**, who went about doing good and healing all who were oppressed by the devil, for God was with Him (Acts 10:38).

We notice in the above verse that Jesus was *anointed* by God. The anointing always has a source, and that source is God. What was Jesus anointed with? He was anointed with the Holy Spirit *and* power. While we all would clearly understand that Jesus was anointed with the Holy Spirit, we need to also see that Jesus ministered with *power*. The Holy Spirit is all-powerful, and He is able to flow His power through His vessels of ministry. I'll be honest with you, I love when the power of the Spirit comes upon me to minister. It makes all the difference in the world. It brings within my spirit-man a confidence in God that is necessary to move into the miraculous. In order for the Church to be more successful in seeing larger numbers of sick people healed, we are going to have to be anointed with the Holy Spirit *and* power. The anointing of power is a perceptible anointing that can be sensed or felt.

> *Immediately the fountain of her blood was dried up, and she felt in her body that she was healed of the affliction. And Jesus,* **immediately knowing in Himself that power had gone out of Him**, *turned around in the crowd and said, "Who touched My clothes?"* (Mark 5:29-30)

Jesus knew that power had gone out of Him. He knew within Himself that the power had gone into someone. People often ask me, "Brother Steven, can you sense when the power flows into someone when you lay your hands on them?" The answer is yes, I can. The knowing comes from within. It's not something that can be analytically explained, but is rather an unmistakable, inward knowing that energy, or power, has flowed out of you. This is quite often perceptible as well by the person receiving the anointing.

I can also sense when someone is not receiving the anointing. Sometimes there is something present that is blocking the flow; often it can be pride, unbelief, or refusal to forgive someone. Often those in a healing line are not only receiving a physical miracle, but a miracle of inner healing as well. When a person comes into contact with God's anointing, it has a way of tenderizing his or her heart. The presence of God softens hard hearts and allows them to more easily yield to the Spirit's work. As a heart surrenders to the Lord's will, the physical miracle is many times instantaneous. Because of this dual working of physical and spiritual healing, we need to be sensitive to take our time when ministering to those in need. We don't want to rush, just as a surgeon would not rush through a delicate operation.

Endnotes

1. See "mashach"; http://www.studylight.org/lex/heb/view.cgi?number=04886.

2. See http://www.docstoc.com/docs/2167540/Biography-of-John-G-Lake.

CHAPTER THREE

My Testimony

Over the years, many friends and ministry partners have often asked me to share with them how the Lord put me in the ministry. Upon sharing my testimony, they afterward always encourage me to please tell this story to others so they too can be encouraged. Normally, I feel uncomfortable talking so much about myself. But since the Lord receives honor in His ability to redeem broken lives, I will share my testimony and will boast of God's great goodness and His power that transformed me from living in a pit of despair to a place of security and blessing in Him. The anointing of God's Spirit has the power to remove every burden and destroy every yoke. As we yield to God's Spirit and receive that anointing, we will go from victory to victory.

I grew up in church all of my life. My parents took me and my brothers to church every time the church doors were open. We were there Sunday morning, Sunday night, and mid-week service on Wednesday night. We were saturated with "church" as much as possible. But even though I was in church so often, I still was never "born again." I had a lot of religion, but it was dry and void of emotion, especially of joy. The church I belonged to did not believe in using musical instruments. We were told by the preacher that to use a musical instrument in church would cause us to go to hell. So there was never a piano, guitar, or anything to help create an uplifting mood. All the songs we sang were from an old hymn book that glorified a future joy in Heaven while living a life of suffering and misery while on the earth. It wasn't much to get excited about, but we got through it with some creative and imaginative thinking.

Because I went to a small-town church, my brothers and I would have to take turns leading the congregational singing. As teenagers, I remember one Sunday morning my older brother was assigned to lead the singing. We always sang the same old songs over and over again. To break the monotony he told me before the service, "Today I'm going to sing 'Bringing in the Sheaves.' But I'm going to change the words and instead sing 'Bringing in the Cheese.'" I said, "You're not really going to do that, are you?" He smiled and replied, "Sure I am, nobody will ever know the difference." Sure enough he got up there and led the whole congregation in singing as we all stood and sang three full stanzas of "Bringing in the Cheese." Well, we never did bring in any cheese, or sheaves to my knowledge, but we got through another meeting!

In the church I grew up in, the preacher's last name was Rich. He was called Preacher Rich by the church members. Even though his last name was Rich, he appeared to be one of the poorest preachers I ever met. Not only was he poor, but the church took great pride in his poverty. They considered him to be extra holy because he was so poor. They gloried in his poverty and in the fact that they did not believe in tithing. The church wanted him to be poor because they thought it was a sign of holiness. (We had no idea it was a sign of ignorance.) By keeping the pastor poor, the church members had no clue they were sabotaging their own means of blessing. God's blessings flow from the head down (see Ps. 133), but they had dishonored their pastor, and thus proverbially shot themselves in the foot. This dishonoring of God's servant caused widespread poverty and financial lack among the majority of the congregation.

The teaching that "God wants you to be poor and have none of this world's goods" was a message I heard often. As I grew up to be a young man, the seeds of that teaching lay dormant in my heart until a time in which the devil launched a well-planned spiritual attack upon my life. In 1991, I had a dramatic experience with God in which I received the baptism in the Holy Spirit. All my life I had been taught by the church I attended that miracles were not for today and that God no longer performed miracles of any kind. But when I was filled with the Spirit and spoke in tongues while visiting a small Pentecostal church, I discovered that God was truly a miracle-working God. My spiritual walk with God began to progress quickly as I wanted to learn about all the wonderful things in the Bible. I did make great strides in breaking free from old sin habits, but I still did not have a strong foundation of basic biblical truths to stand on that could help me be a success in life. Eventually I felt it was time to transition to a different Pentecostal church. I stayed in this other church for some time and learned some additional truths that were helpful, but I was still not made aware of solid biblical New Testament teaching that would renew my mind. Most of the messages I heard were based around the subject of salvation, but I was already saved so it was like watching re-runs on television every weekend. It was essentially the same thing over and over again. It was at this time, when I was in my early twenties, that the enemy pulled the trigger on me in an attack that was meant to destroy my life.

One day I went to work and upon arriving at my job, I was met by the boss. He informed me that I was being laid off from work due to the company downsizing. Because I had been there for the shortest period of time, I was the first to be let go. I drove home that same day and discovered that my car began to have some serious mechanical problems. The vehicle was 24 years old and needed major maintenance, but I did not have the extra money to fix the car. I tried to find a new job, but I didn't have any success in my endeavors. Before I knew it, I had fallen behind on my rent and still could not find work. Things seemed to be spiraling downward beyond my control. I was sharing rent in a home with a Christian brother. His father, who was unsaved, owned the house we were living in. One evening I told my friend that I still had not found a job and that I wasn't going to keep letting back-rent pile up on me. I decided I would move out and stay in my car, and then when I got a job and had the extra money, I would return and pay his father the past-due rent that I owed. I packed all my belongings into my car. It wasn't difficult to do because I owned very little. After packing the car, my friend said to me, "Where are you going to go, and where will you stay?" I said, "I don't know; I guess I'll just figure it out as I go." As I drove off, I had no idea what I was going to do.

As I left the home I had been staying in and drove through town, I took a turn down an alley that passed behind a grocery store. At the back end of the loading dock, I saw a large cardboard box. The box was large, as if something the size of a refrigerator had once been in it. Something impressed me that the box could prove useful. I pulled my car over and left the engine running. I didn't like to turn off the engine because the car would rarely start once shut down. After taking a good look at the box, I folded it down and squeezed it into the trunk of my car. I then drove out of the city for about ten miles and saw a nice secluded area that was in a big field. I turned off the paved road and drove across the field. The grass in the field was about five feet tall, and I could hardly see where I was going! I drove until I came into a small opening where there was a small grove of trees with a little gully that had a spring running through it. I noticed a railroad track that crossed over a bridge that spanned the gulley. It was a rather picturesque-looking place. I thought, "Well, I guess this is going to be home for a while."

I turned off my car engine and took out the cardboard box. Underneath the trees seemed the best place for my new home. The trees provided some shelter which was helpful because my cardboard box had four walls and a floor, but no roof! This was not a luxury cardboard box home; this was the modest version that offered a built-in sun and moon roof. It didn't take long to finish the interior decorating. I had one old bed comforter, one pillow, and my Bible as my sole possessions along with the clothes on my back. When I got into the box I found there wasn't even enough room to stretch my legs out, which got uncomfortable rather quickly. Often when I have shared my testimony I have had people come up and ask me, "Brother Brooks, was that fun? It sounds like an extended camping trip." My answer is that it was fun for about two days, but then the fun soon disappeared when there was no food, no money, and no shower. The creek offered my only means of water. It didn't taste particularly good either, and I didn't know where it was flowing from or if it was contaminated, which I'm sure it must have been to some degree.

After four days had gone by, I began to get very hungry. In the trunk of my car I had one can of beans that belonged to me when I lived in the former house. I started a campfire to heat the beans up and planned on eating them right out of the can. The only problem was that I had no can opener. After much work, I finally got those beans opened up by smashing the can repeatedly against a rock. The campfire was now nice and hot, and those beans sure tasted good, even though they had been squished beyond recognition. After that meal, I went three days with no food. I had eaten only one small can of beans in seven days.

As my appetite grew, I decided late at night to walk all the way into town as my car was completely broken down now. I walked the alleys and checked the dumpsters of the local pizza restaurants. In this process, I discovered that if the restaurants had any left-over pizzas at the end of the night, they would throw them in the dumpsters. This was how I survived during my cardboard box experience. Most of the nights there would be no available food. Only about once every four nights would food be thrown out. So the method was eat one day, fast three days, and then repeat the process. Despite this being one of the lowest points in my life, I nevertheless learned the art of prayer and fasting. Even today when the Lord calls upon me to fast, it is never a struggle or a strain. Time went by in my cardboard box, and days passed. I lost all track of time. I didn't know if it was Sunday or Thursday. After awhile, I didn't even know what month it was.

People have asked me, "Brother Steven, why didn't you keep trying to get a job?" My response was that I repeatedly tried. Because I was so hungry, I especially tried to get work at all the fast-food restaurants. I turned in applications at all of them. Often the manager would ask me for my telephone number so that I could be called in case of being hired. This was way before cell phones were in existence. I could only tell them I had no phone number. Then they would say, "Well, how are we supposed to contact you?" I didn't know what to say. It didn't seem to make good sense to tell them, "To reach me, drive ten miles out of town, pull off the road, and look for the cardboard box by the bridge." It was like being stuck between a rock and a hard place. Poverty is a natural and spiritual problem. It can only be overcome through the *known truth* of God's anointed Word. My natural problem was a result of a spiritual deficiency of having never been taught that God cared about meeting one's material needs. I had no faith or expectancy that God could or would help me to get a good job or to earn a solid income. This lack of spiritual understanding produced the outward natural problem of lack and poverty.

Others have asked me, "Why didn't you try to get help?" My response was that I did try. Before I drove out of the city to start my cardboard box adventure, I went by the Spirit-filled, tongue-talking Pentecostal church that I belonged to. The pastor was there, and I sat in his office and explained to him my distressing financial situation. As a young man, I desperately wanted help and counsel regarding my dilemma. He nonchalantly looked at me and said, "Brother Brooks, you must be going through a Job situation. God tested Job in the Bible, and this is something you are going to have to go through." I replied, "Why do I have to go through this? Is this something you have ever had to go through?" He replied with a nervous urgency, "Oh no, Brother Brooks. *This is your own special calling.*" He encouraged me to cooperate with *the will of God.* At that time, I didn't have enough Bible sense to know that I was actually cooperating with the devil.

There were also family members who could have helped, but if I turned to them I knew they would only help me *if* I would denounce the baptism in the Holy Spirit and speaking in tongues. That simply was not an option for me.

There was, however, one possible hope that I tried as a last resort. On the far side of town there was a family relative who was the vice president of a Christian university. This was my last option and seemed to hold forth a ray of light. With great effort, I drove my car to the college and barely made it, due to the engine repeatedly shutting down on me along the way. As I entered the building in which he worked, I was greeted by the receptionist. Politely I asked if Dr. L. was in and if I could possibly speak to him. Surprisingly, he was available, and the secretary showed me in to his private office.

Dr. L. greeted me with a businesslike demeanor as he asked me to sit down and share my reason for coming by. He was a busy man with many students to oversee at a fast-growing and reputable university. Without wasting time, I got right to the point and shared with him the dilemma that I was in. In my appeal for help, I made sure to share my efforts of looking for a job, even though I had not had good results. I asked if there was any work that I could do, and if he knew of a place I could possibly stay temporarily until I got back on my feet.

As I shared my situation with him, he looked at me without saying a word, as he seemed to be silently evaluating the words I was speaking. When I finished, he slowly leaned back into his large, executive leather chair and with a frown said, "What's wrong with you young people that you can't get your act together?" His response stunned me. Being a near relative, I expected at least some compassion, but he offered no help. He concluded the short conversation by saying, "It is up to you to work out your own problems." Whew! It was a low blow. As I stood up to leave his office, I apologized for taking his time. When I left his office and walked across the parking lot to my car, I felt like an absolute, total failure in life. As I looked at my old, run-down car and noticed how badly my clothes were worn out, I asked, "Lord, what is wrong with me that I cannot do anything right?" My discouragement was echoed by the continual hunger in my stomach. It was at this point that I decided not to ask again for help—from anybody. I could not risk revealing my awful situation only to be rejected again.

As I sat in my car on the far side of town, the thought came to me of my old post office box that was nearby. It had been a long time since I last checked it. Shortly before my cardboard-box experience began, I opened up a post office box at a small mail packaging store. Because I paid up front for a full year of usage, I thought that perhaps my post office box might still be open and have something in it. There would be no logical reason to check it now because I had never got anything important in the mail before.

Despite the great discouragement I felt from the meeting I just had, I decided to drive and check my mail. When I arrived at the mail center, I found the key on my keychain to my mailbox. With my rarely used key, I opened up the mail box and noticed an overabundance of junk mail. As I sorted through the mass-mailed flyers and insignificant papers, I unexpectedly came across an envelope from the federal government. I opened it up, and to my surprise there was a tax refund check made out in my name for $400.

This was completely unexpected. I held the check in my hands and thought, "Lord, what am I going to do with this?" As I pondered on this, my mind recalled the past due rent that I still owed my former landlord. The amount that I owed was exactly four hundred dollars. It was now late in the afternoon, so I quickly went to a store to cash my check and drove over to the house where I used to live. My former roommate was still living there. When I knocked on the door, he was shocked to see me. He was even more shocked when I handed him four hundred dollars in cash. I asked him to please give it to his father.

Having paid off that debt lifted my spirit a little higher than before. Incidentally, it was much later in life when I ran across this same former roommate. He told me that the day I left with unpaid back rent his father counseled him on the phone and said, "Son, I want to teach you a lesson in life. Trust me; you will never see him pay that money. You cannot trust anybody in life, so always take care of your needs and don't be concerned about others." The father wanted to use that specific experience as a lesson to demonstrate to his son that it is pointless to expect anything positive in life. But when this Christian brother gave the money to his non-Christian father, it deeply touched the father's heart. I was told the father said, "That beats anything I've ever seen in life." The fact that I repaid the debt touched his heart. The fact that I repaid it while being a homeless person living out of a cardboard box caused him to have to reevaluate the way he viewed the Church and Christianity. It is my prayer that he found the Savior and received eternal life.

The situation that I found myself in continued to get worse. Before I knew it, the season had changed, and winter began to draw near. The leaves soon began to fall off the lush green trees, and the cold winds began to blow quite consistently. By this time, the car had been parked for quite some time and had shut down on me completely. Numerous times I tried to start it up, but there was no success. As I lay in my box, I would sleep with all my clothes on and put the thin comforter blanket on top of me. It didn't help much to keep the cold out. The difficulty of starting a campfire in the cold proved to be mentally draining. The smell of smoke from previous campfires was heavy on me. At times I would wash my clothes in the creek, but this also became increasingly difficult in the winter. The regularity of being cold, dirty, and hungry began to set in.

One night the temperature really began to drop quickly. The wind was howling, and I was absolutely miserable. In order to escape the wind I grabbed my blanket and went and sat inside my car. The car was cold as an icebox, but at least I was no longer in the wind. Although my car wouldn't start, I was able to put the key in the ignition, turn it backward, and switch on the car radio. The radio could only pick up AM channels. Soon I found a channel giving a local weather update. The announcer on the radio could be heard saying, "It's going to be a cold one tonight. The temperature is dropping, and we have a wind-chill factor below eighteen degrees. Stay inside your homes and stay warm!" Turning off the radio, I pulled my blanket over me and knew it was going to be a long night.

That night as I lay in the car I became extremely cold. The fact that I had eaten hardly any food for days certainly didn't help my situation. After lying there for some time, I could feel my toes and feet begin to grow numb. It was at this time that I heard what unmistakably sounded like an audible voice. It was a male voice, speaking in a low monotone: "Tonight you are going to become the first human popsicle in L_____ County. You are going to die tonight, and you will be found dead, frozen in your car." Well, it didn't take a genius for me to realize that was the devil talking to me. That night I fought with all my strength to sit up and stay awake throughout the night. Finally, after a great struggle that lasted for hours, I saw the sun begin to gently rise and break over the horizon. The sun brought much-needed warmth, and I fell off to sleep in complete exhaustion.

Although the weather did warm up a little over the next few days, it soon turned cold again. As the temperatures dropped below freezing, the stress factor in my life began to mount higher and higher. One night I sat in my cardboard box underneath the trees. It was bitterly cold, and I had been trying to read my Bible, but I was too cold, hungry, and overall uncomfortable to concentrate. I closed my Bible and prayed, saying, "Lord, I don't understand why I have to go through this. If you want me to be poor so that it makes me holy, then by this time I should be the holiest man in the state of Texas! But if I am, I sure don't feel like it." With deep frustration, I then said, "Lord, it just can't get any worse than this." As I said that I looked upwards and as I did, I felt droplets of water begin to fall on my face. It had started raining—it *had* gotten worse. For me, that was the final straw that broke the camel's back.

I took my Bible and threw it down in anger. I said, "Lord, somebody has lied to me. This cannot be Your will for me to suffer needlessly like this." My heart broke, and I began to cry, saying, "Father God, please deliver me out of this mess." I know that God looked down from Heaven that night and heard my prayer. He will always answer when we pray in accordance with His will. Up until this time, I had been cooperating with the will of the devil. This was due to having been wrongly told through misinformed preachers all my life that God wanted me to be poor. Now I was ready to cooperate with the revealed will of God. The angels must have breathed a sigh of relief and said, "Thank God, Brooks finally got the revelation!"

The next morning I woke up in my car where I had gone to sleep to escape the rain. For the first time since I had been homeless, there was now an expectancy within me for something good to happen. As I prayed that morning, the Holy Spirit gently spoke to my heart and gave me instruction regarding my situation. He said, "Do you remember that one particular church that you attended a few times in which you heard good teaching that was new to you?" (The good teaching was that it was God's will for you to be in health and to prosper.) "There was a cell group of that church that met in a home, which you attended a few times. I want you to go back to that cell group that is meeting tonight at 7:00 P.M., at the same home." This brought back to my memory a very good church that I had visited only a few times before. I could also remember the cell group that the Holy Spirit mentioned to me.

I said, "Lord, I will go back there, but I have a problem with my car. It won't start." The Holy Spirit spoke to my heart and said, "You just get ready, I'll take care of the car." Before I left for the meeting I went down to that little stream and washed my hair and tried to clean up as much as possible to remove the thick smell of campfire smoke. Washing your hair with just water and no shampoo doesn't clean very well, but I looked a little better than before. Now that I was ready I grabbed my Bible and went and sat in the car. I said, "Lord, this car hasn't started for a long time, but I thank you for getting me to that meeting." I turned the ignition forward and stepped on the gas, and smoke blew out of the muffler. The car was alive again! I backed it into reverse and drove through the meadow with grass so tall that it reached above the rooftop of the car. Within a few minutes I was back on the paved road, and I put the pedal to the metal and burned rubber. After driving for about 20 minutes, I arrived in the neighborhood of where the house meeting was at. Intentionally, I parked my car two blocks away and around a curve so that no one would see my clunker. Not only was the car a bomb, but sitting out in a field for so long had caused it to become completely covered with a thick, oily dust that the rain couldn't wash off. I didn't want anyone to mistake me for driving a vehicle that looked as if it belonged to the Beverly Hillbillies or the Adams Family.

After parking my car, I walked to the house and entered inside. There I sensed the sweet presence of the Lord and could feel the warmth of Christian fellowship. Some of those already there recognized me from when I had come before. One person greeted me and said, "Hey man, we haven't seen you for a while. What happened to you?" I smiled and replied, "Oh, I've been kind of tied up lately."

As I walked toward the living room where the meeting was being held at, I passed by the kitchen along the way. There sitting on the kitchen counter was a tall glass pitcher of pink lemonade and a plate full of sugar cookies. Since these refreshments were put out to be eaten, I decided to refresh myself and not let any go to waste! Within a few minutes I had drank several full glasses of lemonade and eaten about a dozen cookies. Because I had not eaten any food in three days, the massive sugar rush caused me to be wired full throttle throughout the entire meeting. I didn't miss anything that happened that night; I was buzzing the entire time.

As the meeting began, we sang songs of praise and worship, and then the speaker was introduced. There were about 25 people present in the room that night. The speaker was an evangelist named Steve P. This minister gave a good sermon, and about 30 minutes later he concluded his message. He then made an announcement that within a few weeks he would be traveling to South America to share the Gospel and to carry medical aid to those in need. He then said he would receive an offering that would go toward this trip. An offering basket then was brought forth and began to be passed around the room. We had all been sitting in a circle with the evangelist standing in the middle of us.

As the basket began to come around the room the most unusual thing happened to me. Even though I had been homeless and eating out of dumpsters and trash cans, I had always saved four one-dollar bills in my wallet. They were kept there because I figured if I was going to die, then at least I could walk into town and buy one final meal at McDonald's before I went under. Those four one-dollar bills were all I had and were my final safety net. As the basket got closer to me, I distinctly heard a voice over my right shoulder say, "Give your four one-dollar bills into the offering." As I pondered for a second or two on that statement, another voice on my left side spoke, saying, "If you give them, you will starve to death." It reminded me of those Tom and Jerry cartoons where an angel and a devil would tempt Tom the cat to do something bad to Jerry the mouse. What was I to do? I thought for a brief moment, and then a light went on inside my heart that identified the last voice as that of the devil. Underneath my breath I said, "You stupid devil, I'm already starving!" I reached down, pulled out my wallet, grabbed those four one-dollar bills, and just as I did the offering basket was placed in my lap. I threw those four one-dollar bills into that offering basket and watched as it continued on down the line. When it circled back around to where it began, the evangelist was there to receive it. He held it in his hands, prayed over it, asked God to bless it, and then closed the meeting. Just that quickly it was over.

The people began to slowly stream out, but I left quickly, not wanting anyone to see me drive off in my car. As I walked around the corner and got in my car, I was pleasantly surprised that it started up again with no problem. On the drive out of town, it was difficult knowing that others were going home to a nice, warm house, while all I had was a box in the woods. The devil bombarded my mind with thoughts of discouragement. But even though my natural circumstances had not changed one bit, I felt a peace in my heart that encouraged me.

As I pulled off the road and drove through the field, the devil piped in again and said, "You should have never given that offering. Now you will go under for sure." I said, "Devil, listen to me. If I go under, I will go under knowing that I obeyed God! And because I obeyed God, I don't believe He will abandon me!" The words came out of my mouth with authority, and the devil left. That night I went to sleep hungry, but I dozed off with a knowing in my heart that I did the right thing.

The following week passed quickly. Several times I tried to start the car to go into town to check the dumpsters, but the car would not start. I had to walk into town, but it was a good week as I found more pizza then I could ever eat. Even today, people ask me what my favorite food is—I'm sure you know. Before I knew it, a week went by, and Thursday morning had arrived, which was the day the home church group was meeting. As I prayed that morning, the Holy Spirit again spoke to my heart and said, "I want you to go to that house meeting again tonight." By now I knew the routine.

That day I got ready to go, and when the evening approached I went to my car and sat in the front seat. It was not like I had some kind of super faith. This time I was afraid to turn the key and start the engine. I knew that earlier in the week it didn't start after multiple attempts. Eventually, I turned the key forward really expecting for nothing to happen. But as I turned the key, the car started up again with the entire engine rattling and shaking. I wasted no time and plowed my way through the field of giant weeds and grass toward the paved road. I arrived early to the meeting, about ten minutes before it started.

As I entered the home, I took a seat on a couch toward the back of the room. By this time, after having endured being homeless for such a length of time, my mind felt like it was about to snap. Just as a rubber band can be stretched over and over again until it eventually breaks, I felt that I had reached the breaking point before suffering a total mental breakdown. Sitting on the couch, I found it difficult to smile and continue the game of pretending everything was OK. Looking up, I saw the minister, Brother Steve P., enter the room and walk over to me. He gently extended his arm toward me and placed his hand on my shoulder. As he did, a warm feeling went into my body that dispelled the spirit of hopelessness away from me.

I immediately reacted by reaching up and grabbing his arms. "Brother Steve," I said, "I need to talk with you." He smiled compassionately and said, "Let's go into a back room so we can talk privately." We went to an adjoining room of the house, and he closed the door behind us. As I sat on a bed, I said, "Brother Steve, I don't know how to explain my problem to you." He joyfully said, "Oh, just go ahead and tell it." Sensing trust and a genuine care, I opened my heart and began to pour the whole ugly matter before him. I said, "Brother Steve, I've been living out of a cardboard box and eating out of trash cans and dumpsters..." And I just broke into tears as the story just poured out of my heart.

Brother Steve put his arm around me. He looked me in the eyes and said, "Steven, if you will go out there and tell the people what you just told me, God will do a miracle in your life." Thoughts quickly raced through my mind of what the people would think of me if they really knew my embarrassing situation. However, I was willing to do whatever I needed to do to end the misery. Looking at Brother Steve, I said, "Will you stand with me when I tell them?" With confidence he said, "Yes."

We stood up and walked to the door, and when Brother Steve opened the door, all eyes just turned and looked directly at us. Again, there appeared to be around 25 people in the room. As we stood in the doorway, he said to the people,

"Brother Steven wants to share something with you." That was my cue. I looked at the people, paused for a moment in an attempt to compose myself, and said, "I want you to know I've been living out of a cardboard box, and eating out of trash cans and dumpsters and…" At this point, I completely lost all composure again and began sobbing uncontrollably. As I stood there with tears flowing and everyone looking at me, suddenly a young woman in her early twenties shouted out, "Let's take up an offering for Brother Steven!"

When she said that Brother Steve motioned for me to go and sit down in the middle of the room, within the circle of people who were there. I sat on the floor and crossed my legs and closed my eyes. I wasn't sure exactly what was taking place, but after a few seconds of sitting there somebody threw something, and hit me in the head with what they threw. I thought, "These people are crazy!" But I kept my eyes closed and decided to go along with whatever they were doing. Then, from another direction, something had hit me in the head again. It didn't hurt, but I sure was wondering what was going on. Within a few seconds I felt like I was in a popcorn popper, things were bouncing off of me everywhere. Something was also being stuffed into my shirt pocket. After two or three minutes when the commotion stopped, I opened my eyes and there was cash money all over the floor.

They had been throwing money at me. The evangelist came over and kneeled down next to me with a big bucket like you would see at a fast-food chicken restaurant. He said, "Let's gather it all up and go in the back room and count it." We scooped it all into the bucket and went into the side room while the rest of the group sang praise songs. Brother Steve took that big bucket and poured out the money on the bed. We spread it out and started counting it together.

The first thing I saw was a $20 bill. We added it up as we went along: $20, $45, $80, $120, $180, $220. Brother Steve stopped for a moment, looked at me, and said, "This is a good offering for a small group like this." Then we continued counting: $280, $310, $370, $400. After counting all of it, we reached a total of $418.

Then he stopped and looked at me with authority in his eyes. He said, "Do you know what this is?" With a puzzled look, I responded, "No." He said, "This is the hundredfold return!" Then looking at me with earnest intent, he said, "I want to ask you a question. Did you give four one-dollar bills into the offering last Thursday night?" I said, "Yes, but I didn't think anyone knew about it." He said, "My wife saw you give it. This is the hundredfold return." I then vaguely recalled reading about the hundredfold return in the fourth chapter of the Gospel of Mark.

That night I received $418 to help get me back on my feet. But that's not all that happened. I was also offered a room in the home of a businessman who was in the meeting that night. He made a pledge not to charge me any rent for the first three months. Praise God. But that's still not all. The same businessman hired me immediately to go to work for him with a full-time job. In one night, God delivered me out of the pit of despair, poverty, and hopelessness. That job also ended up being a tremendous experience that worked out extremely well for both me and the other businessman. Even today, the memories of that job are sweet.

The Lord is able to deliver a person out of anything. Since then, I have shared my testimony countless times and have discovered that the Holy Spirit is well able to remove any burden and destroy any yoke. Today, my life is a completely different picture from those earlier days of being homeless and living in a cardboard box. God has given me a wonderful wife and children. He placed me into the ministry and has blessed every area of my life. My greatest desire is to serve Him and honor Him in all I do. The Lord cleaned me up on the inside and on the outside. Over the years I have meditated on the hundredfold return that Jesus spoke of.

> *But these are the ones sown on good ground, those who hear the word, accept it, and bear fruit; some thirty-fold, some sixty, and some a hundred* (Mark 4:20).

While I certainly believe God can multiply back literally 100 times more, I believe the more complete meaning is that the hundredfold return represents *God's very best for you*. If you will honor God with your best, He will honor you with His best. God will even change your present calling or assignment to a much higher level if there is a corresponding deeper surrender and willful obedience.

It used to puzzle me when Jesus taught on the hundred-fold return because numerically it didn't make sense to jump from thirtyfold, to sixtyfold, and then to one hundredfold. It's obvious that from 1 to 30 is an increase of thirtyfold. Then from 30 to 60 is an identical increase of thirtyfold. You would think Jesus would then mention sixtyfold to ninety-fold increase, but He doesn't. So, what's the reason for the break in the divine pattern?

Late one night I was waiting on the Lord in prayer. After a considerable time in prayer, I began to meditate on the meaning of the thirty-, sixty-, and one hundredfold increase. I lifted up a question to the Lord, and simply asked, "Lord, why did You skip past ninetyfold increase and go to one hundredfold increase?" Just as clear as day, the Lord spoke to my heart and said, "Because I am too much!" Whew! That made an impact on me when the Lord spoke those words. Over the years, I've learned that Jesus is not only able to meet needs, He likes to exceed them, sometimes by extravagant measures. We need to set our hearts toward God and pursue His best for our lives. Our aim should be nothing less than the hundredfold return.

Chapter Four

An Unexpected Visitor

While ministering across the country in our motor home, I always used to enjoy going to this certain RV Park while in Southern California. Lots of memories of the Lord's faithfulness float through my mind when I think about the many times I stayed there in our motor home. That was years ago, and we now fly to all of our meetings, but we used to travel throughout the states in our motor home. It was an effective way to do ministry until our schedule got to a place where we had to travel faster. The park in which we stayed was a beautiful park, and dozens of motor homes from around the country stayed there year-round because of the warm weather. There was a winding river that flowed along the park's boundary, and each day I would find a quiet place along its bank to sit down in a lawn chair and pray.

In the previous chapter, I mentioned that in the summer of 2006 the Lord placed an anointing upon my life for miracles of healing. After that took place, I began to see sick people constantly healed in our meetings. This actually caught me off guard because miracles were happening with such ease that I was searching for a clearer understanding of the overall picture of this sudden change.

For about a week, the Holy Spirit impressed upon my heart to seek the Lord for a better understanding of the healing anointing. Because we were traveling from church to church, we actually arrived back in Southern California for various meetings in the area. We decided to check into the same RV Park with which we had become so familiar. One night while there, I awoke in the motor home at 3:30 A.M. My wife and daughter were peacefully sleeping, but I found my spirit was stirred to pray. Very quietly I tiptoed out of the motor home and sat in a lawn chair beneath a covered canopy a few feet from the motor home. It was a beautiful night, and the stars were brilliant. I could hear the nearby river slowly flowing by. All was peaceful, but at the same time there was an "electric" sensation in the air. I knew something supernatural was about to happen.

I glanced down at my watch and it said 3:33 A.M. I knew that prophetically indicated the famous verse found in the Book of Jeremiah.

Call to Me, and I will answer you, and show you great and mighty things, which you do not know (Jeremiah 33:3).

When I looked up, I saw to my right what appeared to be some type of portal, or spiritual dimension that began to open up. As it did, light began to stream forth through its opening, and the Lord Jesus walked out from it and came and stood five feet in front of me. The Lord also had an angel that stood with Him on His left side. When I saw the Lord, I was so thrilled in my heart. With joy I said, "Lord Jesus, I've been wanting to talk to you about..." Before I could finish my sentence, the Lord had already read my thoughts, and said, "I know, that's exactly why I've come to talk with you." The Lord already knew I wanted to better understand the anointing, so He got right to the point. He said, "Tell the people, that when you lay your hands on them and My anointing flows through you and then into their bodies, tell them it works the same way as if someone had an infection, and they were given an antibiotic." Jesus then paused for a moment, so I could let that statement sink in.

He then continued speaking. "The moment the anointing goes in, it will destroy the sickness or disease. Sometimes the results will be instantaneous. Other times the manifestation will occur within two, six, or eight hours later. When the anointing is received with faith, it will always produce results." The Lord then reminded me of the time 12 years earlier when I had a case of strep throat. I had contracted such a severe case that it literally felt like my throat was raw and on fire. After several days of excruciating pain, I couldn't endure the pain any longer and decided to go to the doctor. He gave me a powerful shot of an antibiotic. The moment the shot of antibiotic was administered into my body I knew I was healed. Moments after the shot my throat still burned and the pain was still fully there, but I knew the strep throat virus was being neutralized and destroyed. Within 30 minutes all the pain was gone! It was such an immense relief.

Jesus then reiterated to me that His anointing works the same way. The anointing of God's Spirit is an antibiotic that destroys sickness and disease. After Jesus finished talking with me, He and the angel seemed to slowly disappear from my sight. The last thing I saw was Him smiling at me. I stayed awake for another hour pondering on the words that Jesus had just spoken to me, and then I went quietly back into the motor home and went to sleep. When I woke up in the morning, the first thing Kelly said was, "You had a visitation last night, didn't you?" She never saw anything but knew in her heart that the Lord had come to me.

It's amazing how many times I have seen people receive miracles when I pray for them and the healing takes place just as Jesus described to me. For instance, a few weeks ago I hosted a conference in my hometown, and we had a wonderful meeting. Some people came from the local area; others drove or flew in from other states. One lady in particular came from Alabama needing a miracle. She flew to the meeting in faith that God would do what the doctors could not do. Both of her kidneys had failed, and she needed a transplant. There was a long waiting list in front of her for transplants, so her situation did not look good. This woman was being poisoned to death because of the kidneys not operating. The kidneys are what filter toxins and waste products from your body. That night I laid hands on her and prayed for her, and the anointing of God flowed into her. As I had my hands on her

I saw a vision, and I saw the hand of the Lord reach inside her body and touch her kidneys. I then told the woman exactly what I saw. She left the meeting that night and went back to her hotel room, which was convenient because the meeting was being held in the hotel ballroom. As I closed the meeting that night, I invited all those staying at the hotel to join me for breakfast the next morning. That's always fun to do because it gives us a time for fellowship.

As I went down to breakfast the next morning, the first one to say hello to me was the woman from Alabama. She looked at me and said, "I'm healed!" I said, "I believe you are, but something tells me you have verification." She said, "I do have evidence. I have a Jewish doctor who has been overseeing my situation. He spoke to me recently while in his office and he said, 'Now, I know you believe God to give you a miracle. I can understand that because I believe in miracles. Should you receive your miracle, you will know that you are healed when you begin to urinate profusely.'"

This dear woman told me that after I prayed for her she went back to her hotel room after the meeting and laid down to go to sleep. After two hours, she had to get up and go to the bathroom. She said, "I have been urinating all night and all morning long!" Her kidneys were fully operating and were busy flushing out all the waste that had accumulated. I believe she got new kidneys. That's not just a healing, but rather a creative miracle.

I have seen the Lord heal countless people instantaneously when I have prayed for them, but there are many times when the healing manifests hours later. We also see this in the ministry of Jesus.

Then as He entered a certain village, there met Him ten men who were lepers, who stood afar off. And they lifted up their voices and said, "Jesus, Master, have mercy on us!" So when He saw them, He said to them, "Go show yourselves to the priests." **As so it was that as they went, they were cleansed** (Luke 17:12-14).

These ten men were lepers. According to Levitical law, lepers were to be stoned if they came within 100 paces of a healthy human. So they stood at a distance when they called out to Jesus. It's remarkable to see that the lepers were not cleansed until after they *went*. Their act of going to see the priests, while they still had all the symptoms and conditions of lepers, was their demonstration of faith. Many today do not receive their healing because when they receive prayer, they then look at their body and say, "It doesn't look or feel like I'm healed, so I guess I'm not." Therefore the anointing does not work because it is not mixed with faith. When the lepers obeyed the words of Jesus, *they were healed as they went*. So this was not an instantaneous miracle, but one that occurred later on *as they went*.

Just as Jesus told me in the vision that there would be both instantaneous and progressive miracles, I see many instances in my meetings of those who are healed *as they go*. One such situation happened a little over a year ago in a different conference I hosted. In this conference, I was very busy because not only was I hosting it with international speakers and hundreds in attendance, but I also was speaking in the meetings as well. One woman had flown to our conference in North Carolina all the way from California. She had an accident and broke five bones in her foot. She was on crutches and had a protective soft cast on her foot. She arrived at the beginning of the conference and stayed for each meeting, which lasted a total of three days.

Each day an usher would come to me and remind me that this woman came to the meeting because she wanted me to pray for her foot, but I was so busy that I never did get to pray for her. On the last day of the conference, one of my assistants came to me in the afternoon and said, "Steven, this woman is still waiting for you to pray for her. She's outside waiting right now." I replied, "Oh my goodness, I completely forgot. Please tell her I will come out right now and pray for her." My assistant looked at me with a sad face and said, "Steven, she has brought a pair of tennis shoes, and she plans on wearing them back on the plane when she flies home." My assistant was letting me know this in an attempt to convey that this woman had gotten her hopes up and that we needed to let her down gently so she was not discouraged when she flew back with her foot still shattered and in pain.

However, the report had the opposite effect on me. When I heard that this woman came with a pair of shoes to wear home, then I knew she came in faith. I could hardly wait to pray for her. I went quickly to where she was at, laid my hands on her, and asked God to completely heal all five broken bones in her foot. The anointing flowed into her body and foot as smooth as silk. She was ready to receive. I then left because I had to get ready for the final meeting that evening. When I left, there was still no noticeable difference in her foot, but I knew God had touched her.

We had a wonderful service that night. As the conference came to a close around nine o'clock P.M., I asked our praise and worship leader to close out the conference with one more praise song. As we all lifted our voices and praised God together, here came that dear woman dancing down the aisles toward the front before the whole audience! She was completely healed! Glory! She was dancing in the Spirit, and it blessed everyone there. No crutches, no rubber cast—she had taken it off, stepped out in faith, and acted upon the anointing that was administered earlier. I'm here to tell you that she did wear those tennis shoes on her plane ride home. Nothing is impossible with God.

A few weeks later, I talked with her on the phone and asked her what the doctor said when she went in to have her foot reexamined. She said the doctor took new X-rays and said, "It appears that you did not originally break five bones. You broke seven! But I have never in my life seen such phenomenal new bone growth development!" This woman and her mother both have the before and after X-rays, with the X-rays after the miracle of her foot showing "white streaks" where the new bone growth shot out. My friend, she was healed *as she went*. The problem with many people is that they never *go*. Many sit and analyze. But there is a place in God when you act upon the anointing, and thus receive.

The Church is learning to respect and honor the anointing. In the vision I mentioned earlier, Jesus told me, "Tell the people…" He was emphasizing to me the importance of communicating to the people that He has anointed me with a miracle healing anointing. Why would the Lord do this? Because faith (for a need to be met) comes by hearing (that someone is anointed to deal with that situation). Those who received miracles through the Lord's ministry were the ones who recognized Him as being anointed of God.

I've often taught from the Gospel of Mark, which shares with us the story of when Jesus went to minister in His hometown of Nazareth. Jesus had ministered in other towns with remarkable results. I'm sure if there was any place where Jesus desired to see people healed, it would be His hometown. These people knew Jesus because He grew up there, had previously worked there as a carpenter, and would have had many relatives there. When Jesus taught in the synagogue on the Sabbath day in Nazareth, the people marveled at His teaching ability. They were amazed at His knowledge of the Law. They were in wonderment, but they were also perplexed as to how this could be.

Instead of recognizing who Jesus really was, they began to reason and dissect Him to pieces. They could not get past the point of their "local boy" being the one whom God had anointed. Despite the report of miracles in other towns, they begin to show their contempt by calling Him *the carpenter* and the *son of Mary*. I want you to know that God can take a janitor, high school dropout, trash collector, or chimney sweeper, and by His grace deposit His anointing upon that person to accomplish greatness. They still tried to label Jesus as just *the carpenter*, but He knew who He really was. Often when you develop in your walk with the Lord, you encounter those who made the decision never to move forward. They still talk the same low-level way. They don't understand the change in you, and they personally have no desire to ever change. They try to hold you down and crush your dreams. But you must always believe who God says you are.

Because the majority of the people of Nazareth rejected Jesus, they also rejected the anointing that was upon Him.

They shot themselves in the foot. They lost a golden opportunity because the Anointed One didn't come in the kind of package they were looking for.

> *Now He could do no mighty work there, except that He laid His hands on a few sick people and healed them* (Mark 6:5).

Jesus did everything in His power to try and get the people to believe, but often the old saying, "You can lead a horse to the water, but you can't make it drink," proves true. It wasn't the Lord's fault those people did not receive miracles. Jesus was anointed. He was ready. But the people failed to connect with the anointing upon His life. It works the same way today. It doesn't matter who the minister is, or where the ministry is taking place. Whether it's in America, Africa, Asia, or Australia, the minister has to endeavor to get the people to *believe* in God's willingness and ability to perform miracles, and in the presence of the anointing to produce miracles. That's why Jesus said to me in the vision, "Tell the people…" If people don't know that God has anointed me in this area of healing miracles, then I tell them so that they can release their faith in order to receive. If they already know, then I have a platform of faith already established.

God is placing fresh oil upon His people. God is positioning your heart to receive a deep impartation of the Spirit's oil. Let us now explore more closely the composition of this sacred oil that we may better understand the hidden mysteries associated with the anointing of God.

CHAPTER FIVE

Spice Up Your Life

Moreover the Lord spoke to Moses saying: "Also take for yourself quality spices—five hundred shekels of liquid myrrh, half as much sweet-smelling cinnamon (two hundred and fifty shekels), two hundred and fifty shekels of sweet-smelling cane, five hundred shekels of cassia, according to the shekel of the sanctuary, and a hin of olive oil. And you shall make from these a holy anointing oil, an ointment compounded according to the art of the perfumer. It shall be a holy anointing oil" (Exodus 30:22-25).

Aren't you glad that the God we serve is never boring or unable to fascinate our spiritual and physical senses? God is full of variety and creativity. The holy anointing oil could only be made through a highly skilled master perfume maker who was responsible for using the finest ingredients and the most exacting measurements. God choose certain plants that are now known for creating some of the most famed spices in the world. God did not tell Moses only to use oil for the purposes of anointing the sacred items. But we see that the anointing oil was *spiced* with highly fragrant and aromatic oils that when all combined together produce a substance that is beautiful and complex. That's the way God wants our lives to be.

We were not created to be born into this world, live a miserable life, work an uninspiring job, eat, sleep, and then one day die and go to Heaven. Our life on this earth should revolve around a passionate desire to live life to the fullest. I'm not talking about sky-diving or jumping off a high bridge with a bungee cord tied to your ankle. I'm talking about the fragrant life that is produced by *knowing what you are here for* and *pursuing that God-given destiny with all your heart.* Many thrill seekers are doing ridiculous stunts these days because they have a spiritual emptiness on the inside of them, so they endeavor to appease that through reckless and life-endangering behavior. I want to tell you right now that if you want a life of high thrills, adventure, and journeys into the unknown, then step out in faith and follow God's plan for your life! Not somebody else's plan. Not your best friend's plan. But follow God, and He will take you on a journey that will flavor your life with enough spice that people will look at you and say, "Wow, that guy (or gal) is living their dream. What an example!"

Spice is used to enhance the quality of whatever it is added to. Back in the Bible days, most of the food was rather bland. Unless you were a king, you ate plain, basic food, which could get boring very quickly. Those of royalty had access to regular meat and bread. But if all you had was beans, rice, and vegetables, then you were faced with eating that three times a day for most of your life, except for a wedding or a special holiday. That's why spices were so highly valuable back in those days. The food may have always been the same repetitive meal, but spices open up endless flavor possibilities.

Many people might think that the process of making the holy anointing oil was a simple one. It would appear that all you would have to do was gather the listed plants, grind them into spices, measure out the exact proportions, and then mix it in with the olive oil. However, it is not so simple. By following the process just mentioned, only a thick, gooey mess would be produced.

*And you shall make from these a holy anointing oil, an ointment compounded according to the **art of the perfumer** [apothecary]. It shall be a holy anointing oil* (Exodus 30:25).

The rabbis teach that the process was much more intricate then just mixing some ingredients together and putting them into a bottle of oil. The task required an apothecary whose skill was making fine perfumes. This was not an assignment for a novice or someone who only had a recreational interest in the matter. It appears that the fresh ground spices were softened in water and boiled in a delicate procedure in order to extract their essence. The spice essence was then mixed with oil and myrrh and boiled *again* until all of the water had evaporated. The perfume makers could be better described as chemists, with extensive knowledge of plants, herbs, flowers, and trees. Only a skilled perfume maker would have the ability to create the sacred anointing oil in its purest form.

Once I spoke in a conference that was held on the very top of the Mount of Olives in Jerusalem, Israel. The Holy Spirit impressed upon me to teach on the fragrances of Christ. I took my text from the classic verse found in Psalm 45:8.

> *All Your garments are* **scented** *with myrrh and aloes and cassia...* (Psalm 45:8).

The word *scented* is not used in the original Hebrew language. You could translate this verse literally as, "All your garments—myrrh, aloes, and cassia."[1] The garments of the King were so saturated with these costly spices that it appeared as if He wore a fragrance for His clothing! After I finished speaking and ministering during my session, I walked out of the meeting area to have lunch. As I did so, a dear Christian brother who I had never met before from Australia came cheerfully up to me with great joy in his heart. He said, "Brother Steven, that was a beautiful message you just taught. It blessed me in a special way because I work for a perfume company, and our best-selling product is patterned after the exact verse you taught on." He then sprayed some of the fine fragrance onto my arms. Glory to God, it sure smelt wonderful. I walked around for the rest of the day smelling like myrrh, aloes, and cassia.

The composition of the holy anointing oil gives us tremendous prophetic insight into the realm of God's Holy Spirit. One who is anointed by God is one who understands how to move with the Holy Spirit. What greater joy can there be in life than to be able to work in harmony with God? The first thing we notice about the anointing oil is that it is extremely holy. *Holy* in Hebrew is *kodesh*.[2] When something is *kodesh,* it is to be set aside and kept separate. This means it now has the power to sanctify and elevate everything around it. For example, in the nation of Israel you may hear the phrases *Eretz HaKodesh* (the Holy Land), *Yerushalayim Ir HaKodesh* (Jerusalem the Holy City), *Beth HaMikdash* (the Holy Temple), or *Kiddushin* (marriage sanctity). The Jewish rabbis teach that these designated holy sites and values have the power to elevate and infuse everything around them with holiness. In the Old Testament we see that marriage, the land of Israel, and the Temple were considered holy. But the anointing oil was considered *Kodesh HaKodashim*, which means "Holy of Holies"![3]

Again, we see that the anointing of God is not just representative of the Spirit's power, but is also very holy and sacred. The Torah was explicit regarding the punishment of the misuse of the anointing oil:

> *Whoever compounds* [mixes] *any like it, or whoever puts any of it on an outsider, shall be cut off from his people* (Exodus 30:33).

Because of its elevated status, it had to be extra carefully guarded against misuse. My friends, I want to tell you a truth right now. If you are anointed by God, you have got to stay on your alert against that old devil. The devil isn't that concerned about troubling sinners. He knows he already has them. But he wants to take down those who are anointed because they pose a tremendous threat against his kingdom of darkness. The anointed ones are those with the power to induce heavenly change. You have to be careful how you use the anointing. The devil will tempt you to misuse it, to draw attention to yourself, to exalt yourself, to manipulate others through a divine gift. When the anointing is in operation, it will always attract attention, but it is how it's handled that matters. The glory must always be directed fully to the Lord.

There are four fascinating spices used in the making of this oil. They are:

Liquid Myrrh—500 shekels

Sweet-smelling Cinnamon—250 shekels

Sweet-smelling Cane—250 shekels

Cassia—500 shekels

Olive Oil

A shekel was about 12 grams in weight, and a hin was about 16 fluid ounces. If we were to convert those measurements into our modern-day equivalent, this is what we would get.

Liquid Myrrh—25 fluid ounces

Sweet-smelling Cinnamon—12 fluid ounces

Sweet-smelling Cane—12 fluid ounces

Cassia—25 fluid ounces

Olive Oil—16 ounces

Let us now begin to study the ingredients in the anointing oil and draw upon the prophetic revelations that God has placed within the Scriptures.

ENDNOTES

1. See http://biblelexicon.org/psalms/45-8.htm.

2. See "kodesh"; http://www.studylight.org/lex/heb/view.cgi?number=06944.

3. See http://www.chabad.org/library/article_cdo/aid/144745/jewish/The-Holy-of-Holies.htm.

CHAPTER SIX

Liquid Myrrh: The Suffering of the Godly

Liquid myrrh is drawn from a cultivated plant that grows in the Arabian Peninsula, among the countries of Oman and Yemen. Ancient trade routes ensured that this product was exported to Israel, as well as to many other countries. This plant grows as a small tree or shrub to a height of usually nine feet. Myrrh has many uses because it is a natural astringent. I use a toothpaste and mouthwash containing myrrh, and it produces a wonderful, deep but gentle, cleansing sensation that even affects the gums.

In the ingredients for the anointing oil, we see that myrrh is listed first. This is because myrrh is a *fixative oil*. It has the ability to preserve the fragrance and potency of other spices. Only a master perfume maker would know this. God knew exactly what He was doing.

The myrrh tree produces a resin that flows from the tree when deliberately cut. This process is known as *milking the tree*. A sharp knife or axe is used to make incisions into the bark of the tree. As the sharp instrument cuts into the tree, a milky resin that exudes outward begins to harden as it is exposed to the air. The hardened droplets are known as *tears*. About two weeks later, the *tear collector* gathers the droplets from the trees and takes them to the merchant to be sold. Myrrh is a beautiful prophetic picture of our Lord Jesus because it represents sufferings and unjust persecution that we all experience in our walk with Him. The Lord Himself carries the fragrance of myrrh.

> **All Your garments are scented with myrrh** and *aloes and cassia* (Psalm 45:8).

Myrrh has a natural bitter taste. So does suffering. None of us get excited about suffering, but there are times when the Lord takes us through such experiences for our spiritual development. If we are to be fully developed with the fragrance of Christ emitting from us, then we will at times have to taste suffering. I'm not talking about suffering something that Jesus redeemed us from while on the cross, such as sickness and disease. But I am speaking of the suffering that comes through the process of our being formed into the image of Christ.

> *For it was fitting for Him, for whom are all things and by whom are all things, in bringing many sons to*

glory, **to make the captain of their salvation perfect through sufferings** (Hebrews 2:10).

Just as the myrrh tree sheds tears when cut, we too feel the sting of verbal and emotional abuse from those who cut at us with sharp tongues. Jesus sees the tears that flow; He is very familiar with the process. The shortest verse in the Bible is *"Jesus wept"* (John 11:35). The tears Jesus shed that day were not tears of sadness due to the death of His dear friend Lazarus.

I'm sure it saddened the Lord to see the consequences of sin so prevalent in the earth even thousands of years after Adam's original transgression. Jesus surely had compassion on those suffering that day, but there's a hidden truth in Jesus crying when moments later He raised him from the dead. I believe the primary reason Jesus cried that day was because no one around Him, not even His close friends Mary and Martha, believed He could raise a man up who had been dead four days.

You'll notice when Jesus went to raise Lazarus from the dead that the Scriptures tell us *He groaned in the Spirit.* It deeply pained Jesus that not even those closest to Him truly understood his identity as the source of all life. When Jesus asked them to roll away the stone, most of the people by that time thought He had surely lost his mind.

> *Martha, the sister of him who was dead, said to Him, "Lord, by this time there is a stench, for he has been dead four days." Jesus said to her, "Did I not say to you that if you would believe you would see the glory of God?"* (John 11:39-40)

Jesus knows the pain of being misunderstood. Jesus has tasted the bitterness of not being accepted by His own people. Jesus could not escape the rejection of even His own brothers and mother who thought He had gone mad.

For even His brothers did not believe in Him (John 7:5).

While He was still talking to the multitudes, behold, His mother and brothers stood outside, seeking to speak with Him. Then one said to Him, "Look, Your mother and Your brothers are standing outside, seeking to speak with you" (Matthew 12:46-47).

Perhaps the Lord's mother (Mary) and His brothers were there to "talk some sense into Jesus." Who knows, maybe they had already contacted a good psychiatrist they wished to refer Him to. If it happened to Jesus, don't think people aren't going to give you those funny looks at times, either. We see clearly a similar response in the following verse.

"Then the multitude came together again, so that they could not so much as eat bread. But when His own people heard about this, they went out to lay hold of Him, for they said, "He is out of His mind" (Mark 3:20-21).

The religious leaders attacked the Lord's sanity from a different angle. They accused Jesus of being demon possessed....

And the scribes who came down from Jerusalem said, "He has Beelzebub," and, "By the ruler of the demons He casts out demons." (Mark 3:22)

Just because Jesus experienced suffering did not mean He went around sad and discouraged. We are told in Scripture that Jesus was *anointed with the oil of gladness* (see Heb. 1:8-9). Many years back, a much older and seasoned minister told me, "Steven, to be successful in the ministry you have to have a heart like a lamb and skin like an elephant." That's an amusing statement with quite a bit of truth in it. We have to discard hurtful things and not hold on to them. If you hold on to the wrong done to you and develop resentment, it will eat you up on the inside. Just let it go; God has a better plan.

When the Lord began to call me into the ministry, I was very faithful to study the Bible for hours at a time. I studied the teachings of respected ministers and did all I could to *study to show myself approved* (see 2 Tim. 2:15). After my day at work, I would open up my Bible and surround myself with study guides, concordances, biblical encyclopedias, and any other spiritual tool I could get my hands on. I even learned classical Greek and could read the New Testament in the original language. I could do this for hours because I was single at the time and lived a very simplified life. However, I thought something was missing because other people I knew who desired to be in the ministry all went off to Bible college or seminary.

After considering the paths that others were taking, I quickly decided that I would do the same. The Spirit of God never directed me to go, but in my mind I simply thought, "This is what I must do because everybody else is doing it." So, with good intentions I set off to join a Bible college. I even moved to a town with a good, Spirit-filled Bible college in order to attend that school. I arrived three weeks before the school session began. I did not have enough money to enroll, but I trusted that in the three weeks the money would come in.

While there I felt it would be best to find someone with whom I could share an apartment in order to save on expenses. After asking quite a few people, I finally found one individual who could help. He already had an apartment and was waiting for classes to begin. He had paid his tuition in full and was living by himself in an apartment with an extra room that he was not using. This brother also had a personal written letter from his pastor recommending him as being most worthy of acceptance into the ministry. Becoming his roommate at the time seemed to be a good fit as I didn't have any other options. I agreed to pay him on a weekly basis, and I then moved in.

As the time grew nearer for the first semester to begin, I was still far short of the needed funds. I gradually felt a growing distance in the relationship with my roommate as he saw my financial dilemma and appeared to delight in it. As the final days ticked away and the money never appeared, his behavior turned from condescending speech to abusive speech. He began to *cut* into me with such statements as, "It's obvious you are not called into the ministry, or else you would have your money for Bible college." Or he would say, "It looks like you are going to miss out on all the fun; *you* are just not qualified like *the rest of us.*" Whew! I tell you he made some pretty good cuts into the bark of my tree. I could feel the myrrh flowing out. I wanted to prove to him that I *was called* and that the Lord *did have* a place for me in the ministry, but all he could see was my inability to go forward. Eventually the deadline came and went, and my tuition money never came in.

As the semester began without me, I was forced to pack my bags and get ready to go back home. On my final day in the apartment I was loading up my remaining items. I suppose my roommate thought it fitting to drop in and to give me one final verbal gouging before not seeing me again. He entered the room and looked at me with a false smile and somberly said, "I'm sorry it didn't work out for you. I'm sure you must be disappointed because of your failure. Well, I've got to go; my friends are waiting for me at the special luncheon for all the new students. Goodbye." Having said that, he turned around and walked out, while shutting the door behind him on purpose with a tremendous slam. I could hear him laughing to himself as he walked off down the hallway. We all taste bitter experiences sometimes in life, because bitterness (myrrh) is a required ingredient in the anointing oil.

It was a rather perplexing situation as to why the Lord didn't open the door for me to attend a Bible training college. After a period of time, the Lord did speak to me about it, but not until I was already in the ministry and preaching in churches. One day while in prayer the Lord spoke and said, "It was not My will for *you* to attend a Bible college. The school you endeavored to attend was a good school, but I had a different plan for your life. The curriculum they were teaching was based on books you had already studied, and you were well ahead of where they were beginning at." That blessed my heart when the Lord shared that with me. Notice the Lord said it was not His will *for me* to attend a Bible college. That doesn't mean it's His will for *others* to do the same. We have to follow the plan that God has for us individually, because it is different for each person. Without question, God has raised up schools of ministry, Bible colleges, and seminaries. Because He established these, it is also His will for certain persons to attend and study there.

Years went by, and I found myself preaching in churches all across the country and in different nations. The days of the endeavor to go to Bible college and the verbal buzz saw episodes with my former roommate were long behind me. I never did let it bother me, and I chose to forgive that person in my heart and go on with God's plan for my life. The years passed, and my ministry continued to grow. One day I received an invitation to minister in a very well-known church. This church is known internationally, and the pastor is a great man of God. To speak in this church is an honor. Some of the most well-known speakers in the world have also ministered here. Now it was my turn.

The Sunday morning on which I was to speak proved to be a beautiful day. The sun was shining, and I knew in my heart that God was going to perform miracles in the service. As I arrived at the church, I was taken immediately to the pastor. We talked for a moment in his office, and then he said, "Steven, I've assigned someone to serve you and take care of all your needs while you are here. If there's anything you need, just tell him what to do." The pastor left to attend to a few things before the service started, and I was then left alone. It was at that point that my "servant" came in to serve me a glass of water. As he came in, I instantly recognized the servant as my old roommate! He said, "Hey, Steven, how are you doing?" He was so kind and gracious to me. He previously read on the church bulletin of my coming and anticipated my arrival. He never made a verbal apology to me for the things that happened years ago, but it was not necessary to do so. The apology was written in his eyes with a look that expressed what he knew had now become evident, that God had lifted up Steven and given him an *international ministry*. I never once said anything to him about the things he said; I had truly forgiven him and moved on. But his life was a different story.

Despite having gone to a Bible college, he was still not in the ministry, His position there in the church was only as an assistant, and he had only been there for a short period of time. That day he graciously carried my Bible, opened my water bottle, and saw God do supernatural miracles in the meeting. It didn't elevate my head or make me turn with an attitude and say, "Well, that sure shows you, doesn't it!" There was no axe to grind or any desire in my heart other than to see my brother in the Lord progress in his walk with God. Perhaps this brother was at this moment going through his own myrrh experience that would prepare him to advance in his calling. These experiences were all part of the process that God chose for me to go through. When God found it fitting to redeem that situation, He did it in *His timing*. Although tears of myrrh were once shed, a new fragrance of joy was now there to sweeten the experience. It happened well over a decade later, but God is not in a rush when creating the correct spices needed for the anointing oil.

CHAPTER SEVEN

Sweet-Smelling Cinnamon: The Upright and Joyful Life of the Believer

The next spice we see mentioned is sweet-smelling cinnamon. It is considered by many to be the most popular spice in the world. This is a spice I enjoy because of its beautiful fragrance *and* taste. I always love drinking a hearty, robust mug of chai tea because of its wonderful notes of cinnamon. Wherever I travel in the world, I also am constantly looking to discover the world's best cinnamon roll. I eat them not just for breakfast but any time I can find them. When I find a good cinnamon roll, I don't waste any time; I always eat the center part first because it has *more* cinnamon than the outside layers. Anything with cinnamon in it seems to lift my spirit and make me happy. Cinnamon speaks to us primarily of *joy*, which is probably why this spice is so well liked around the world, because everyone loves to be happy. It also reminds us of the benefits of living a life that is *upright* before the Lord.

In contrast to the inward bark of the tree, the outward flowers of the cinnamon tree produce an unpleasant smell. As a symbol, this characteristic of cinnamon suggests the world's inability to comprehend how we have joy in Christ even though we may experience persecution, difficulties, or hardships.

> *Blessed are you when they have insulted and persecuted you, and have said every cruel thing about you falsely for my sake.* **Rejoice, and be exceedingly glad,** *for great is your reward in the Heavens; for so were the prophets before you persecuted* (Matthew 5:11-12 Weymouth).

The joy that God gives goes far beyond just being happy. Some people are happy when they go out to shop for new clothes, or eat at a favorite restaurant, or experience moments when all is well. But the joy that God gives is much deeper than simple happiness, which can be influenced by the time and the moment. Joy that originates from God is more than just being in a good mood. *Joy is a spiritual force.*

> *Then he said to them, "Go your way, eat the fat, drink the sweet, and send portions to those for whom nothing is prepared; for this day is holy to our Lord. Do not*

sorrow, **for the joy of the Lord is your strength"** (Nehemiah 8:10).

The joy of the Lord is your strength. When that joy comes upon you, it makes you not only thank God for His personal blessings that we richly receive, but it also makes us mindful of others: *"and send portions to those for whom nothing is prepared."* Giving to others in need increases our joy. Some people have lost their joy despite great personal blessing. One of the ways to recover joy is to give to others.

In many of the nations where I minister, there are churches that cannot afford to pay my airfare to come. Yet the Lord places it upon my heart to go teach them the Word of God. Not only do I go, but I bring my wife and daughter with me. That's three international airfare tickets that have to be paid for. I'm glad I serve a big God. I have traveled all over this world while bringing my wife and daughter along. There's a big element of sowing in that. My own ministry is supported by some of the most wonderful ministry partners who *give generously* to make this happen. Each year I make sure I accept some invitations from churches or ministries who greatly desire that I come and minister to them but financially cannot afford the airfare. It's my way of giving *to those for whom nothing is prepared*. Because I do not exclude the poor, God has richly blessed me.

Biblical joy can be in manifestation in a person who is going through a great trial. The unsaved person has no revelation of this type of reality. It can only be experienced in Christ. There is nothing this spiritually dead world has to offer that can surpass the level of joy that a Spirit-filled believer can tap into. The highest level of living can only be discovered in living fully in and for the Lord Jesus.

Cinnamon also improves the flavor of those things that taste bitter. The contrast of bitter-sweet experiences gives a glimpse of the mosaic that can be seen in the life of the Lord Jesus. Because we are *in Him*, we also will have similar experiences in which we come into contact with godly suffering and joy.

The cinnamon spice we eat actually comes from the dried bark of the tree. The word *cinnamon* comes from the Hebrew word *qinnamown,* which derives from an unused root meaning "to erect."[1] The bark of cinnamon trees comes off in *upright* roles. You have probably seen these rolls of cinnamon sticks in hot apple cider beverages during the cold winter season. The upright sticks speak to us of the Lord's righteousness. We are the righteousness of God in Christ. When God the Father looks at you and me, He sees us as being in Christ; therefore, we are considered righteous. To be righteous is to be in right standing with God. This is a position we receive based on the Lord's redemptive work at Calvary. The upright rolls of bark from the cinnamon tree also speak of living an upright life in an experiential way that reflects our identification in Him. Righteousness not only expresses a position, but also should outwardly demonstrate godly living.

We live in an age when there is an assault on all that which is holy. A *culture of grunge* seems to have invaded the Church. The Church desperately needs strong and loving leadership that will, in particular, steer the younger generation in the right direction. In the church in which I was mentored (by a very godly pastor), there were spiritual mothers in the church that would help the younger woman and new female converts in the faith. If a woman came into the church knowingly or unknowingly with cleavage being exposed, the spiritual mothers would respond to that. They might say, "Oh, honey, it looks like you forgot your blouse," and then they would hand that woman a temporary covering. They would do it in a way that was not condescending, but it would still gently get the point across.

A great disservice is done to the young believers today when they are encouraged to wear crude clothing that looks like they have been living homeless out on the street. When a young man or woman wears pants that expose parts of their rear end, they need to be mentored. They don't need another pizza party or another trip to the amusement park. They need a spiritual father or mother who is willing to help them move past their current level of understanding.

When I was much younger, I used to be heavily involved in martial arts. For a span of 12 years, I trained on a regular basis under the leadership of some very capable, mature men who were master instructors. Never in my years of training would I step into the training room (dojo) wearing pants that were falling off my rear end. Never did I see the instructors that I trained under degrade themselves by sloppy dress. There was order in those houses. Most of those training halls were known as *houses of discipline.*

Some believers get all excited and say, "We are the army of the Lord!" But an army has discipline. I've been to Arlington National Cemetery in Arlington, Virginia, and I have watched the changing of the guard. It is a tremendous demonstration of honor, precision, discipline, and order. None of those professional soldiers have their shirts hanging out and their shoe strings untied. Their pants aren't torn in shreds, and their hair is not uncombed. Yet some of our young people in church often reflect the complete opposite of standards of excellence. Where is the honor, discipline, and respect that God deserves?

The holy anointing oil was ministered in an orderly and precise way. God gave Moses very specific and detailed instructions pertaining to the usage of the oil. I think it would be highly advantageous for young Christians in America to visit Washington, D.C., at some point in their lives to view the Honor Guard at Arlington National Cemetery. The order and precision demonstrated give us some insight into the strict preparation of the anointing oil. The priests who served in the temple had strict dress code requirements. The high priest wore various assortments of clothing, and it was very important to God that he wear the prescribed clothes and that they even be put on in the proper order. The standard of honoring God needs to be raised in the Church. We see a very high standard of what is required to serve in this distinguished field of being an Honor Guard. The following are some interesting facts of discipline and duties required to serve in the U.S. Army Honor Guard:

- The selection process is very rigorous, requiring a certain look and a strong military bearing.

- It is the second least-awarded badge in the U.S. Army, after the Astronaut Badge.

- To be in the Honor Guard, you must be between 5 feet 10 inches and 6 feet 4 inches tall.

- You must be physically fit and have a proportionate weight and build.

- You must memorize seven pages of history on Arlington National Cemetery and then recite it verbatim.

- You must memorize the grave locations of 300 veterans.

- Each sentinel must keep their uniforms and weapons immaculate.

- You must complete extensive training in the manual of arms, learning the intricacies of military ritual as well as the guard change ceremony.

- Even after completing all training and passing the test for the badge, the right to wear the Honor Guard Badge is only permanent after the soldier has served at the Tomb of the Unknowns for nine months.[2]

God wants to train up a mighty army of young people who will be fully surrendered to do His will. Part of the training will require the instillment of principles that will make them the envy of corporations and Ivy League schools.

Of course, I'm not trying to imply that we need to go to the other extreme and have such strict, rigid order that there is no joy or fun in serving the Lord. But the truth is that it is possible to have the combined blessings of an excellent spirit and a joyful life full of freedom in the Holy Spirit at the same time. God will always honor those who honor Him. The Lord wants the best.

The king of Babylon chose Daniel along with his friends Hananiah, Mishael, and Azariah to go into special training to serve in the royal palace. The king was not looking for misfits or rejects. He wanted the best.

> *Then the king instructed Ashpenaz, the master of his eunuchs, to bring some of the children of Israel and some of the king's descendants and some of the nobles,* ***young men in whom there was no blemish, but good-looking, gifted in all wisdom, possessing knowledge and quick to understand, who had ability to serve in the king's palace,*** *and whom they might teach the language and literature of the Chaldeans* (Daniel 1:3-4).

Today, God wants the best for His end-time army. Yes, God will accept a drop-out or a loser, but He will not leave that person in that condition. The anointing of God's Spirit will transform any life. God is able to make a champion out of a loser, and a winner out of a hopeless case. When I was a young man, I struggled in school. It was very difficult for me to focus mentally and study. My grades were always low, usually just the bare minimum to get by. After school I would stay and spend extra time in remedial study classes to help me grasp basic principles of math, English grammar, and literature. I struggled terribly in those three subjects. Each time I went to one of those classes it felt like torture.

The literature class in particular was beyond my limits of understanding. The teacher would read a story from a book and then ask us to explain what we had just read. All of the students could give correct answers except for me. I simply could not comprehend anything that I read or heard. One day when I was a senior in high school, I finally answered a question correctly. We were assigned to read a story on the life of Abraham Lincoln. The teacher then began to verbally quiz us on what we had just read. All of the other students were answering correctly. The teacher's eyes finally drifted over to me, and she said, "Steven, what was the name of Abraham Lincoln's wife?" All eyes in the classroom turned toward me, and I experienced total brain freeze. Suddenly, I received a flash of inspiration. I shouted out, "Her name was Mrs. Lincoln!" The whole class burst into laughter. The answer was semi-correct, but it was not the answer the teacher was looking for. "Dumb Steven," they all thought, "it's a wonder he can even write his own name."

If it were not for the favor I had as the high school track star, I don't think I would have made it. There was one class that was very difficult for me, which was fortunately taught by one of the school's administrators. This man had the position of being the head administrator over the school's entire coaching staff. During my senior year, our school hosted a regional track meet. Countless schools came, and it turned into one of the biggest sporting events of the year. Our school was under pressure to perform well. The superintendent and other school officials expected our track team to put forth a good show.

The big day arrived, and I was scheduled to race in the two-mile run. Out of my entire track team, I was the school's only hope for a first-place, gold-medal win. As I stood on the starting line, I knew the competition was going to be tough. The race started, and after a few laps, I pulled ahead of the pack with another runner, and we began to battle each other for the win. It was neck and neck all the way for eight laps, but on the final home stretch I pulled ahead and took a hard-fought victory. I'll never forget the moment I crossed the finish line in front of the jubilant hometown crowd. The person holding the finish line ribbon was my teacher, the administrator! As I broke the ribbon in victory, I stopped to catch my breath, and he came up to me with a big smile, leaned over discreetly to my ear, and confidently said, "Congratulations, son, you just passed for the year." I never understood anything he taught in class, but at the end of the year I somehow received a high score. Whew! I needed all the help I could get!

After finishing high school, it was off to college. I was looking forward to running track, but the dread of academic failure still taunted me. With each passing semester, I told myself that I would eventually pull up my faltering Grade Point Average. However, I was greatly disappointed when after four years of college, my academic advisor told me I could not graduate because my GPA was below the required standard. He suggested that I consider taking some *easier* classes in an effort to raise my GPA. (I had already been taking the easiest classes offered.) After staying another semester to give it a try, I found I still couldn't break out of my pattern.

It was then that I decided to transfer to a different college. Once there, I put in a full year striving to pull up my GPA. Finally, after a total of five-and-a-half years in college, my GPA had actually gotten lower! Others had already passed me up, graduated, and attained good jobs because of their college degrees. The writing was on the wall. It was time for me to move on. There are those gifted students who graduate with perfect grade point averages of 4.0. That means that person had all A⁺s on their grade scores. When I left college, my GPA for my final semester was .08! When I later turned my heart fully to the Lord and received the baptism in the Holy Spirit, God was there to receive me just as I was, but He did not leave me as I was.

Today, God has done a transformation in my life. As I consumed large amounts of His Holy Word, it began to change my thinking over a period of time. Honestly, I know it even changed my brain. Now I can grasp things mentally that would have eluded me before. Even scientific literature and mechanical problems are enjoyable for me to read. The hours I spent reading the Bible and in prayer while I prayed in tongues produced a change that transferred outwardly. I have gone on to write books that are now in bookstores throughout America and around the world. My ministry is impacting nations, and God has me speak before multitudes. Truly, God deserves all the glory. It is God's desire to *develop us and to anoint us*, just as he did with Daniel and his three friends.

We should be willing to give God our best. God wants the brightest and most gifted minds to work for Him. He wants those who have an excellent spirit. Have we sold our talented young people to elite government jobs, large executive corporations, and the medical field so that we may be considered successful by the world? If parents find themselves with a gifted child, why don't they consider encouraging him or her to become a minister, instead of a surgeon or an engineer?

Shouldn't the ministry of the Lord Jesus Christ have the best? I ask this question because of the coming end-time harvest in which untold multitudes of souls are going to be swept into God's Kingdom and the desperate need for trained ministers is going to be overwhelming.

> *Then He said to them, "The harvest truly is great, but the laborers are few; therefore pray the Lord of the harvest to send out laborers into His harvest"* (Luke 10:2).

The ministry of the Lord Jesus Christ is about to experience a huge "hiring spree." The call into the ministry is going to be so sudden and strong upon those called that they will do complete 180 degree turnarounds to go in the direction of God's Spirit.

Even if there is not a calling into the fivefold ministry office, that still doesn't excuse an individual from the call to be a soul winner. Every Christian should want to reach as many souls as possible for Jesus within their given sphere of influence.

We should not forget that the majority of "brilliant minds" who produced incredible music and scientific breakthroughs that blessed the whole world were mostly deeply devoted Christians. If God gives you a gift, you should use it for His glory. Don't be ashamed to identify your gifting or your anointing as having been given to you by God. God gives those gifts and abilities to provide a platform of influence to draw others to Him. Let's consider a few quotations from some well-known scientists and musicians as examples of how they honored God and used their notoriety to publicly influence others for Christ.

In 1654, Blaise Pascal (1623-1662) was reading the seventeenth chapter of John when he had a dramatic encounter with God and was mightily baptized in the Holy Spirit. He immediately wrote these words about the encounter and was said to have sewn them into the clothes he wore so that they were always with him:

> From about half past ten at night to about half an
> hour after midnight,
> FIRE.
> "God of Abraham, God of Isaac, God of Jacob,"
> not of philosophers and scholars
> Certitude, heartfelt joy, peace.
> God of Jesus Christ.
> God of Jesus Christ.
> The world forgotten, everything except God.
> "O righteous Father, the world has not known You,
> but I have known You" (John 17:25).
>
> Joy, joy, joy, tears of joy.[3]

Raised as a child prodigy, Pascal was a scientist noted for his work in physics and for developing the first mechanical calculator. He was certainly a mathematician of the highest order. At the age of 12, he was discovered having written on the wall with a piece of coal an independent proof that the sum of the angles of a triangle is equal to two right angles. At the age of 12, he was allowed to sit in gatherings that included the greatest mathematicians and scientists in all of Europe. He endeavored through his notes and letters to refute the idea that to become a Christian you had to "disengage your brain." Although he only lived to the age of 39, he created mathematical theorems that are still used today. Pascal debated the existence of God with the finest minds of Europe, but his emphasis was on knowing God personally, not intellectually.

Johannes Kepler (1571-1630) was a mathematician and astronomer who discovered that the Earth and planets travel about the sun in elliptical orbits. He is credited with discovering the three laws of planetary motion. Kepler also did important work in optics and geometry. This was his testimony:

> I had the intention of becoming a theologian…but now I see how God is, by my endeavors, also glorified in astronomy, for "the heavens declare the glory of God."

> God is the kind Creator who brought forth nature out of nothing.[4]

Sir Isaac Newton (1642-1727) formulated the law of universal gravitation, and was a mathematician, physicist, alchemist, theologian, and inventor of calculus. He also published *Newton's Prophecies of Daniel,* which was based on his study and translation of the book. Through his many discoveries, he relied on the Lord Jesus to reveal the answers to complex problems. He said, "All my discoveries have been made in answer to prayer."

On one occasion, an atheist-scientist friend was marveling at a small-scale model of the solar system that Newton had on display in his home. The model was exquisitely made and was operated by a hand crank that caused the planets to orbit and rotate. When the atheist friend asked who made it, Newton said, "Nobody." His friend responded by insisting that it was certainly made by someone who was a genius. This led to Newton's reply:

> This thing [a scale model of our solar system] is but a puny imitation of a much grander system whose laws you know, and I am not able to convince you that this mere toy is without a designer and maker; yet you, as an atheist, profess to believe that the great original from which the design is taken has come into being without either designer or maker! Now tell me by what sort of reasoning do you reach such an incongruous conclusion?[5]

Sir William Herschel (1738-1822) who discovered Uranus, several nebulae, and binary stars, was also the first astronomer to accurately describe the Milky Way Galaxy. He observed,

> All human discoveries seem to be made only for the purpose of confirming more and more the truths contained in the Sacred Scriptures.

The undevout astronomer must be mad.[6]

George Frideric Handel (1685-1759) composed what many consider to be the world's most beautiful music. *Messiah*, which he wrote in just 24 days without once leaving his house and barely eating any food, contains the famous

"Hallelujah" chorus, of which Handel remarked, "Whether I was in my body or out of my body as I wrote it I know not. God knows." There is a story told that as Handel was writing this chorus, which is drawn from Revelation chapters 11-19, his assistant walked into the room after shouting and looking for him with no response. The assistant reportedly found Handel in tears and sobbing with intense emotions. When asked what was wrong, Handel held up the score to this movement and said, "I did think I did see all Heaven before me, and the great God Himself!"[7] In his last years Handel attended church twice every day. In England church members almost rioted and threatened to break down the church doors to get in and hear the music!

A few days before Handel died, he expressed his desire to die on Good Friday, "in the hopes of meeting his good God, his sweet Lord and Savior, on the day of the Resurrection." He lived until the morning of Good Saturday, April 14, 1759. His death came only eight days after his final performance, at which he had conducted his masterpiece, *Messiah*. Beethoven made the following statement about Handel: "He is the greatest composer that ever lived. I would uncover my head and kneel before his tomb."[8]

Johann Sebastian Bach (1685-1750) is one of the all-time greats of classical music. He once wrote, "The aim and final end of all music should be none other than the glory of God and the refreshment of the soul."[9]

Bach is the German word for a little stream or brook. Beethoven said, "His name should not be Brook; it should be Ocean!"[10] Bach was a composer, an organ virtuoso, and probably the hardest working of all the great musical geniuses.

Bach was a passionate Christian whose personal library was filled with theological works that he studied intensively. On many of his compositions, he inscribed the letters I.N.J. or S.D.G., which stand for *In Nomine Jesu* (In the Name of Jesus), and *Soli Deo Gloria* (To God alone, the glory).

In the examples we have just read, it is wonderful to see such persons use their vocational life calling to glorify God. As I mentioned earlier, there is soon coming an enormous harvest of souls that will flood into the Church. The Spirit of God is moving upon the hearts of many, stirring a desire to begin training for ministry. God is looking for His people who desire to serve Him in ministry and are more concerned with reaching the lost than a job that offers guaranteed health benefits and a 401(k) plan. If God calls you to work for Him, He will always take care of you. God's benefit package is the best. Put God first, and you will be handsomely rewarded every time.

Parents should be open to the idea that God could desire for their children to be ministers. To be a minister of the Gospel of the Lord Jesus Christ is a high calling. A parent should feel deeply honored if God chooses their son or daughter to be a preacher. I know in my heart there are some parents who are reading this, and you are struggling with this revelation. You have made plans for your children to go to a certain college, and you see them going off to medical school or some other esteemed profession. But what does God desire for them? Are you willing to allow them to make their own choice as the Spirit of God leads them? We must be willing to take up our cross and conform our plans and desires to the perfect will of God.

Consider Hannah and how she released her hopes and wishes to God. She was a spiritual woman because her heart was sensitive to God. Hannah was barren and unable to have a child. She was desperate and sought God in prayer regarding the situation.

And she was in bitterness of soul, and prayed to the Lord and wept in anguish. Then she made a vow and said, "O Lord of hosts, if you will indeed look on the affliction of your maidservant and remember me, and not forget your maidservant, but will give your maidservant a male child, **then I will give him to the Lord all the days of his life***, and no razor shall come upon his head* (1 Samuel 1:10-11).*

So it came to pass in the process of time that Hannah conceived and bore a son, and called his name Samuel, saying, "Because I have asked for him from the Lord" (1 Samuel 1:20).

Now when she had weaned him, she took him up with her, with three bulls, one ephah of flour, and a skin of wine, and brought him to the house of the Lord in Shiloh. And the child was young (1 Samuel 1:24).

God gave Hannah a son because she was willing to give him fully to the Lord. She dedicated him to the Lord and God blessed her more then perhaps she could even foresee or imagine. Samuel went on to become one of the most respected and beloved prophets in Israel's history. God wants to take today's young generation and mold them by His Spirit into polished gems that reflect the many facets of who He is. We find many examples of this in the Bible as well as in church history. Take the apostle Paul for example.

Paul was fluent in multiple languages and had a brilliant mind. He was personally taught by Gamaliel, the Jewish doctor of the Law. Paul was an international traveler with interests ranging from religious studies to sports and even to secular poetry (see Acts 17:28). The Lord Jesus prepared Paul to stand before kings and governors to testify of His Name. Paul had a tremendous intellect that was highlighted by his spiritual prowess. Paul moved in the gifts of the Spirit, was caught up to the third heaven, and was a brilliant thinker, preacher, and writer. Paul sets a great case in point to us by demonstrating that you can be intelligent, analytical, systematic (read the Book of Romans, for example), while at the same time being keenly aware of Heaven, angels, and God's miraculous healing power.

Daniel, as mentioned earlier, was also fluent in multiple languages and was a personal advisor to King Nebuchadnezzar. Daniel was deported to Babylon at the age of 16 and was handpicked to serve in the royal palace. He rose to stand in the top circle of a few men who had executive power throughout a nation that was the greatest world power of its time. God gave to Daniel and his three friends knowledge and skill in all literature and wisdom. Daniel was a prophet and was personally granted understanding in all visions and dreams, which played an integral role in his promotion.

> *Then the king interviewed them, and **among them all none was found like Daniel, Hananiah, Mishael, and Azariah**; therefore they served before the king.*

*And in all matters of wisdom and understanding about which the king examined them, **he found them ten times better** than all the magicians and astrologers who were in all his realm* (Daniel 1:19-20).

The ancients of that time were highly advanced in mathematics and astronomy. The area and time frame that Daniel lived in was a cradle of scientific advancement and understanding. Daniel stood at the top of this learning pyramid and was instrumental in receiving and recording major prophetic events.

In our American history, we have the example of Charles Finney (1792-1875) who was intellectually gifted by God in the area of law and justice. Finney was a young attorney practicing law who began to read the Bible in order to gain a better understanding of the judicial system expressed through the Old Testament Law. The more he read the Bible, the more he realized his own need for a Savior. Up until that time, Finney had intellectually believed the Bible but had never made a commitment in his heart to receive Jesus Christ. One day in the woods he prayed and surrendered his all to God. He then soon abandoned his law practice and entered the ministry. I have absolutely no doubt in my mind that we are going to see the same type of sudden career changes in the lives of countless believers as they come upon mighty encounters of God's Spirit.

Finney is responsible for leading over 500,000 estimated people into salvation in Christ Jesus in a time when there were no loudspeakers or modern means of communication. His sermons were powerful, and he called upon people to repent of their sins—even calling out individuals by name!

In one meeting, Finney was troubled that the people were *pleased* with his message. He decided to turn up the heat in his next sermon. He boldly preached the need for conversion and concluded his message by saying, "You who are now willing to pledge to me and to Christ, that you will immediately make your peace with God, please rise up."[11] The Church in Finney's time had never heard or seen a public confession in Christ. The congregation all sat there taken aback by Finney's challenge. Seeing their lack of response, Finney replied, "You have taken your stand. You have rejected Christ and his Gospel..."[12] The congregation was stunned. Finney dismissed the meeting and left. Within a few nights, the entire town showed up, and many souls were saved. Finney's brave but unorthodox methods were effective, culminating at the height of his ministry in revival meetings in Rochester, New York, in 1831.

The Rochester Revival swept through every class of society, especially touching the upper levels of high-society people. Over 100,000 people were considered to have been saved in the revival. Multitudes made open and public declarations of their faith. Nothing was done in a backroom. Religion became the main discussion in every home, business, shop, and office of the city. The whole city was ablaze with a move of God's Spirit. The bars and taverns were closed for lack of customers, and crime in the city was almost nonexistent. The Rochester jail was rarely needed, and the courts had very little to do. God changed Finney's career from an attorney to a minister. Again, I stress that God is calling many into the ministry today because the end-time harvest is so large.

Sometimes people are looking to get into a career that is the next "big thing." The ministry of the Lord Jesus Christ is the next "big thing." God is looking to fill positions. Many Christians need to get on their knees and seek God regarding their career calling. God is searching for the best, and He could very well be searching for you!

Another example of an intelligent mind surrendered to the Lord's service is Richard Francis Weymouth (1822-1902). He produced one my favorite translations of the New Testament called *The New Testament in Modern Speech*. Even now I have my copy on my desk that I read regularly. Dr. Weymouth was a lifetime educator who received his Doctor of Literature degree in 1868 at the University of London. He was the first graduate to receive this particular doctoral degree, and his exam was so difficult that no one else received the same honor until 11 years later. In earning the degree, he was thoroughly examined in Icelandic, Anglo-Saxon, French, and English language and literature. His translation of the New Testament into a more modern, accurate version was the result of over 60 years of studying the Greek New Testament. He was highly trained in linguistics and published numerous papers on the subject of philological research. The widely read author Oswald W.S. McCall said this about Weymouth's translation: "I do not know of a better New Testament translation anywhere than Weymouth's."[13]

I believe we can see in Scripture and in church history that God wants the best players on His team. Why should the devil get the smartest and brightest? If you had your own business, wouldn't you want to hire the best employees? God is the same way. A new standard is being raised in the Church. The Church many times has measured her standard by comparing herself with the world. The Church has looked at the world and said, "I live a little higher than that; therefore, I am doing OK." But we mustn't compare ourselves against those who are spiritually dead. The Word of God must remain the standard that we pursue.

> *In this manner, therefore, pray:*
> *Our Father in heaven,*
> *Hallowed be Your name.*
> *Your kingdom come.*
> ***Your will be done***
> ***On earth as it is in heaven***
> (Matthew 6:9-10).

The way things are in Heaven should be transferred into the way we live our lives on the earth. God is raising the standard, and He is expecting us to lift our sights higher. Honor, reverence, and respect for God must be restored to a higher level in the Church. Older and more mature believers must be willing to lovingly invest their time and efforts particularly into the younger generation along this line. We need to teach and impart the sacred values of holiness:

> *"without holiness no one will see the Lord"* (Hebrews 12:14 NIV).

By the Lord's grace, I have had some remarkable spiritual experiences when the Lord has allowed me to be caught up to Heaven (see 2 Cor. 12:2). In the visitations that I have had, I have never seen anyone walking around in Heaven with their belly button or rear end showing. Nor did I ever see any women in Heaven walking around with low-cut tops exposing their cleavage. *The cult of sloppy dress does not exist in Heaven.* There may be believers who dress that way down here, but Heaven only reflects the Lord's taste, and His taste is brilliant holiness. I have never seen any people in Heaven who looked disheveled or unkempt. There's nobody walking around in Heaven smoking cigarettes or telling crude jokes. It simply does not exist there. The Kingdom of God is void of grunge, filth, sleazy dressing, and every other low-level form of spiritual darkness. The devil is dirty and crude. God is holy and pure. Let us lean toward and embrace the light, not the darkness. Allow your life to reflect excellence, virtue, and divine order.

I know some people will think what I'm writing is not *cool.* Personally, I have no interest in trying *to be cool.* Who wants to join some club that's based on what other misinformed people think about you? Some people want the world's approval while still trying to keep everything smooth with the Lord. But I'll tell you right now that you will never have the world's full approval unless you are willing *to go all the way.* There are no thumbs *up* from the world unless you *sin like them* and *sin with them.* So why is the Church pleading for the world's acceptance? God is sprinkling fiery hot cinnamon on the Church to purge it from its desire to be embraced by the world. Don't compromise. Be a leader and encourage others to aim high for God. Stir in the cinnamon, drink it down, and God will strengthen you to live *upright* in a polluted world.

The fragrance of cinnamon (representing uprightness and joy) is an essential aroma in the anointing oil. We also see a New Testament parallel to this.

*...for the kingdom of God is not eating and drinking, but **righteousness** and peace and **joy** in the Holy Spirit* (Romans 14:17).

Let us now move on to the next spice contained in the anointing oil.

ENDNOTES

1. See "qinnamown"; http://www.studylight.org/lex/heb/view.cgi?number=07076.

2. See http://www.arlingtoncemetery.org/ceremonies/sentinelsotu.html.

3. See http://www.users.csbsju.edu/~eknuth/pascal.html.

4. See http://www.eadshome.com/Sciencequotes.htm.

5. See http://www.eadshome.com/Sciencequotes.htm.

6. See http://www.eadshome.com/Sciencequotes.htm.

7. See http://gfhandel.org/anecdotes.htm.

8. See http://www.musicwithease.com/handel-quotes.html.

9. See http://sfcv.org/learn/composer-gallery/49.

10. See http://chorus.ucdavis.edu/seasons/0607/
    Beethoven%20Notes%20and%20Text-Translation.pdf.

11. For an online version of Charles Grandison Finney's
    Memoirs, see http://www.archive.org/stream/
    memoirsrevchar00finnrich#page/n5/mode/2up; page 63.

12. Ibid.

13. See http://www.wordsearchbible.com/catalog/
    Weymouths_New_Testament_WEY_874.html.

CHAPTER EIGHT

Sweet-Smelling Cane (Calamus): Spiritual Growth

Next we see that *sweet-smelling cane* is also used in the ingredients for the anointing oil. The exact cane being mentioned is the plant known as sweet calamus, which is a reed that scents the air while it grows. God expects us to grow and develop spiritually. The fragrance of Christ emitting through us should scent the spiritual atmosphere around us. *Calamus* is the Hebrew word *qaneh,* derived from the word *qanah*, meaning "to buy, possess, or redeem."[1] Some of the most expensive perfumes in the world have calamus as a base ingredient. It appears that calamus was imported from India, the same country that supplied the spikenard of the Bible. In India we find that calamus is known as "lemon-grass" or "ginger-grass". Perhaps now you recognize this spice in the list of ingredients that can be found in high-end designer fragrances. Calamus seems to be popular now in hand soaps, shampoos, and conditioners found in extravagant hotels. Recently my wife and I ministered at a church that accommodated us in such a beautiful hotel. The bath and shower products were custom made just for this hotel, and one of the ingredients in the shampoo was calamus. I spent fifteen minutes just washing my hair. Glory to God!

Again, calamus is the Hebrew word *qaneh,* which comes from a word meaning "to redeem." Oh, I want to tell you that means a lot to me. Jesus has redeemed us from the curse of the Law, having become a curse for us. Jesus is our redemption. As a child of God, you are not cursed. You are blessed. You are not trying to get blessed. You already *are blessed* because you are in Christ. Upon that rugged cross Jesus took all sin and every product of sin upon Himself. He bore our sicknesses, our pains, our frustrations, our inadequacies, our failures, our lack, our poverty, and every vile thing imaginable. If a person sincerely repents and turns to God, there is nothing that Jesus cannot deliver him or her from. He has triumphed over all!

I'm deeply thankful that Jesus washed me clean with His blood and saved my soul. Not only did He save me, but He rescued me from a life of failure and frustration. I know some people like to act all dignified and project an image of "having it all together," but outside of Jesus, I never had anything together. Without Him, I found my life simply did not work. But it's a different story now that He fully has my heart; He has blessed me, and I am grateful.

When I think about what Jesus accomplished on the cross, I am exceedingly grateful for how He is concerned enough to take care of every area of our lives. When you read through the Book of Second Corinthians, you will see that the context of those two chapters deal with Paul receiving a special offering to take to the church in Jerusalem. Paul describes the *grace of giving* as he communicates to the Christians in Corinth.

> *For you know the grace of our Lord Jesus Christ, that though He was rich, yet for your sakes He became poor, that you through His poverty might become rich* (2 Corinthians 8:9).

Paul told the church in Corinth, *"...you know the grace of our Lord Jesus Christ."* The context of grace in which he is referring to is the grace of giving. Jesus was rich, yet for our sakes He became poor. The question is, "When did Jesus become poor?" Most people respond by saying Jesus became poor when He left Heaven and came to this world. While it is true that Jesus left behind Heaven with streets of gold and gates of solid pearl and came to a sin-filled world, He still did not become poor at that time. Most church people picture Jesus as a poor preacher wandering around with holes in His sandals, holding unorganized meetings, and then having to scrounge off of people just to get a meal. This is what the devil wants people to think. The devil uses this pathetic lie to keep skilled and gifted people away from entering the ministry. The enemy wants you to think that if God calls you into the ministry then you have to take a vow of poverty and be poor. That is a wretched lie, and it is unfortunate that many in the Church don't know the Bible well enough to refute it.

When Jesus was a young child, wise men came to see Him bringing gifts of gold, frankincense, and myrrh. At this time, Jesus was no longer a baby in a manger, but was most likely below the age of two, which would coincide with Herod's announcement to slaughter all the male children under the age of two. The Magi came to the *house* of Mary and Jesus, *not to the manger* in the stable. The Magi were Persian royalty (modern-day Iraq) who came to see the King of kings. They were obviously of important status because they gained an immediate meeting with King Herod. The three gifts given were traditional gifts given by visitors to a king. These were not trinkets, but royal gifts of gold, frankincense, and myrrh that certainly contributed to the well-being of the family.

When Jesus began His ministry, He chose 12 apostles to accompany Him full time. Jesus had the responsibility of providing for the needs of Himself and the 12 apostles. Some of the apostles were most likely married. We know Peter was because Jesus healed Peter's mother-in-law of a fever. So Jesus had a large staff that required a treasurer—Judas (see John 13:29). Why would someone who is poor have a treasurer? Jesus was not poor; He couldn't have been. No one fights over the clothes of a poor person, but soldiers gambled over the outer garment that Jesus wore, which was a garment woven on a loom in one piece, no sewn seams, making it an expensive piece of clothing.

God is a God of abundance. Jesus is not opposed to you and me being wealthy. He is opposed to covetousness and pride, but we can walk free from these temptations through His grace. Several years back I was talking with a Christian friend I saw occasionally. As we crossed paths one day, our conversation drifted to the subject of the economy. He said, "God will meet your needs, but not your desires." I said, "Is that in the Bible?" (I already knew it wasn't, but I wanted him to think about what he just said.) He replied, "I don't know; I've heard people quote it before." In response I said, "Have you ever heard anyone quote to you Psalm 37:4?"

Delight yourself also in the Lord,
*And He shall give you the **desires** of your heart*
(Psalm 37:4)

Upon hearing God's Word, my friend expanded his faith to receive more than just the meeting of his needs. After all, wouldn't life be extremely boring if all we ever had was only our needs met, and not one thing extra that we wanted? What if you wanted a pack of chewing gum, or a drink while at the gas station? What if you never could have *anything* extra? Well, I found out God is into the *extra* business. When you think about the way that God created the earth, you see that God is a God of abundance.

One day as I was enjoying an apple, I felt an unusual interest to do a little research on apples. I was amazed at what I discovered. In my research I found that although most grocery stores only carry four or five varieties of apples, there are actually over 7,000 different types of apples, all with their own unique appearance and flavor. Now that probably makes some people with a miserly spirit upset because they think the extra variety of apples that God created is unnecessary. But God in His infinite wisdom knows that we all have different tastes and preferences. With so much to choose from, you may want to expand your horizons and try something new.

My favorite apple is the Honeycrisp. It's grown locally here in North Carolina, and it is absolutely delicious. It tastes as good as its name. It has a super-crisp texture and is as sweet as honey. Just one is enough to fill me up. They are so big that they can be a meal in themselves. The abundance of God is displayed through His creation. That's why there are also over 3,000 varieties of potatoes, 13,000 types of beans, 7,500 types of tomatoes, and more than 600 types of oranges. The staggering list of variety seen in just fruits and vegetables reveal to us a God who abundantly supplies our needs and desires.

God is helping His children to develop a mind-set of royalty. The Spirit of God is endeavoring to lift us to see ourselves for who we really are in Christ. I'm not suggesting in any way that we are to be "money-minded." In all my years of ministry, I have never begged or pleaded for offerings, or put out ridiculous appeal letters that are solely intended to manipulate people's emotions to give. Then again, I have actually had some believers present their unscriptural belief to me that "preachers should not accept any money," and that "ministry work should be done for free." But in First Corinthians, Paul reminded us of the Lord's command:

Even so the Lord has commanded that those who preach the gospel should live from the gospel (1 Corinthians 9:14).

It amazes me that some people actually think a minister has no right to receive money. Yet, those who criticize preachers for receiving money will at the same time go work a job and expect to get paid so they can also take care of their families. My greatest desire for these misinformed believers who have these critical thoughts would be to see God call them into the full-time ministry. That way they can work 60 to 80 hours a week—as my wife and I often do—and then have people come up to them and say, "It's wrong for you to be paid for what you do." I can't help but laugh a little. It would be fun to see the Lord turn the tables on them. After all, you do reap what you sow. Perhaps some of these very same critics will find themselves behind the pulpit in the near future! It's amazing how fast your theology can change when you actually live the experience instead of theorizing about it from a distance.

God expects us to grow spiritually so that we might walk in the fullness of every blessing that He has prepared for us. I always enjoy going back to churches where I have previously ministered. This allows me to see spiritual growth in the saints as compared to when I last saw them. Ideally, there should be progress made since the last visit.

I have no greater joy than to hear that my children walk in truth (3 John 4).

Walking in the truth typifies the qualities of calamus. Our growth and development in Christ should not have to be announced, but it should be obvious through a continual upward climb of going from glory to glory, and faith to faith. This is the normal Christian pattern of growth, which, when acted upon, brings great joy to the heart of God.

Just as calamus scents the air with its refreshing and soothing fragrance, so should our lives attract others to desire an intimate walk with God. Even as the sweet smelling cane would emit such a pleasing fragrance, it is possible that God can develop the same "sweetness" in us. There are some things mentioned in the Bible that unless they are personally experienced or encountered through some type of tangible way they do not become a reality to us. Please allow me to share a recent example.

While ministering at a church in the Chicago area I came across the kindest person I have ever met in my life. I'm not saying I have never met any kind people, I have met many. But never in my life have I ever met any person as kind as the pastor of the church that I spoke in. Actually, I did not even know that kindness could be developed to such a remarkable level. Everything about this man's character exuded kindness.

This dear African-American man of God was almost 70 years of age. During his life he went through many difficulties, disappointments, and trials. But he refused to allow these experiences to make him bitter. He decided to draw close to God even when he was perplexed as to why tragedy occurred and took the lives of his immediate family. Even when falsely accused and misunderstood for simply obeying God, this man refused to take offense or retaliate in a wrong spirit. The product of his obedience that was developed through certain trials that he was allowed to experience and overcome had produced a harvest of the fruit of kindness that was unlike anything I had seen before. After several days of meetings in this man's church, my wife said to me, "I think this pastor is the kindest person I have ever met in my life." I replied, "I know. I didn't even realize it was possible for a person to be this kind. I had no idea that such sweet kindness could be such a powerful force."

What was the response in my heart after having had an experiential encounter with an attribute of Christ that previously I was not fully aware of? Quite simply, the answer was that I wanted to have that type of fruit in my life also. Do you see how the fragrance of Christ emitting forth from you can attract others to desire more of Jesus? As you allow the Holy Spirit to finely craft and develop you, just as the master perfumer would create the holy anointing oil, you will also express the "sweetness" of Christ that gently radiates outward and is detected by those around you. Allow the calamus, the sweetness of Christ, to be a strong quality of your life.

ENDNOTE

1. See "Qaneh"; http://www.studylight.org/lex/heb/view.cgi?number=07070 ; see "Qanah"; http://www.studylight.org/lex/heb/view.cgi?number=07069.

CHAPTER NINE

Cassia: Reigning With Christ

The final spice ingredient comprised in the holy anointing oil is *cassia*. Cassia is mentioned as a specific fragrance that the Lord Jesus Christ wears on His garments.

> *All Your garments are scented with myrrh and aloes and **cassia**, out of the ivory palaces by which they have made You glad* (Psalm 45:8).

Jesus left the streets of gold and the mansions and palaces made of pure ivory in Heaven in order to come to this fallen world and redeem His own special creation. Jesus left behind the beauty of those ivory palaces, but as He walked the earth, the spiritual fragrances of joy, uprightness, endurance, obedience, and prayerfulness exuded from within Him.

Cassia is easily recognized by its beautiful purple flowers, which speak to us of the Lord's royalty as the King of kings and the Lord of lords. Cassia is related to cinnamon but has its own unique features. It grows in high altitudes of around 8,000 feet in elevation. This speaks to us of the Christlike walk as we endeavor to *seek those things which are above*, and to *set our mind on things above, not on things on the earth.*

When I was a young man, the Lord Jesus filled me with His Holy Spirit, and it turned my life in a completely new direction. For the first time in my life, I knew I had the power to resist temptation and to overcome all the entanglements of sin that constantly harassed me and had previously held me down. Upon being filled with the Spirit and speaking in heavenly tongues, I immediately made great strides forward in my walk with the Lord. All I wanted to do was pray, study my Bible, and be in the church building the moment the doors were open. I lost all interest in the "pleasures of the world."

Upon seeing my new zeal and abandonment of carnal habits, those around me voiced their *concern* for me. Seeing that I wasn't going to change or pull back from what they called *a reckless choice*, those dear relatives set me down for a little straight talk. With deep reverence and grave seriousness, they said, "We believe you have lost your mind, and we are going to pay to see that you get the best psychiatrist in town." I got so happy, I replied, "Isn't that amazing. The whole time I was in church but bound in sin you all thought I was normal. Now that I want to live holy and genuinely serve God you all think I'm crazy. So, please explain to me, who are the ones really living an abnormal life?" They countered with the statement, "But you believe in that *speaking in tongues stuff*. That's of the devil. You have lost your mind!" In my final defense, I said, "You are all correct. I have lost my mind. Thank God, I needed to lose that old nasty thing! Now I have the mind of Christ, and I plan on renewing it daily."

Not everybody can appreciate the smell of cassia that grows in the heights. Some people, even Christians, choose to live carnally minded. Paul told the Christians in Corinth that they were not spiritual but carnal. That means they were governed by their natural senses. In the Book of Romans, Paul said the carnal mind is hostile toward God. Our English word *carnal* is derived from Latin language, and it means "flesh."[1] Literally, to be carnally minded is to be a meat-head. Whew! This refers to those who prefer the rank smell of the world's garbage. I honestly don't know what some Christians are going to do with themselves when they get to Heaven and find that there are no poker tables, no cigar rooms, no swimsuit magazines, no soap operas, no bingo clubs, no contact sports to watch (I heard the groans on that one), no worldly dancing, no beer or liquor stores, along with a list of other favorite earthly pastimes.

Some Christians will be shocked when they get to Heaven and discover the absence of their favorite music. In Heaven there is no gangsta' rap music that degrades women. There is no sad "tear in your beer" music that glorifies evil spirits of self pity and depression. There does not exist one single song in Heaven that glorifies adultery or immorality, which is what the majority of today's country-western music promotes. I grew up and went to junior high and high school in South Texas. I heard enough country music in the Lone Star State to last me a lifetime. The problem is not really the rhythm or beat (although it often sets a negative tone), but the great damage is done through the negative words that glorify bad luck and the "down and out" mentality. You've probably heard the joke about what happens when you play country music backward: you get your wife back, your job back, and your dog back. Glory! I'd rather listen to something that lifts me up, not something that pushes me down. I honestly think today's country-western music is more displeasing to God than head-banging, rock-and-roll music. With hard rock music, there is no disguising the message of lust and crude immorality. But country-western music is often pawned off as being for *good ole' boys and gals*. The devil is more cunning with this style of music by using a more subtle effort to deceive and influence a larger number of people.

There are many different types of music and styles of music in Heaven, but they are all pure and holy. In Heaven there are no dark and gloomy religious songs that paint Jesus as still being on the cross and suffering under the agony of the world's sin. The music in Heaven portrays Jesus in absolute, total victory over all His foes, and He is worshiped as the mighty conquering Lion of the tribe of Judah. We see represented in the spice cassia attributes that speak to us of the Lord's royal dominion and high authoritative position over all things. Jesus is the triumphant king!

It is fascinating to think that Jesus actually wears a fragrance. In meetings around the world, I have been a witness many times when His fragrance would come into the place of meeting. About a year ago, I hosted a local meeting in Wilkesboro, North Carolina, to preach God's Word and minister to the sick. When it came time for me to pray for the sick, the spirit of prophecy came upon me, and I began to prophesy over certain individuals. As I did, the most clear, distinguishable fragrances of coconut, pina colada, and other refreshing tropical scents began to diffuse through the room. Almost every person smelled it, and it would go through the room like invisible waves of glory. It was like we all were just transported to a beautiful beach in the South Pacific islands. Those in the meeting were so uplifted by these refreshing smells. The Lord knows how to lift your spirit and relax your soul. With Jesus, you can have a vacation without ever leaving town!

Once when I was in southern India, there were many people in the meeting sick with infections and open, running sores. As I began to minister, suddenly an unmistakable, overwhelming fragrance swept into the meeting that was identical to the sterile smell you find in modern, clean hospitals. Hospitals use different iodine and alcohol-type cleaners to kill airborne and surface germs. Well, you would have thought somebody took a gigantic bucket of that germicide and threw it over the crowd. Instantly I discerned the fragrance, and the associate pastor next to me stopped and said, "That smells like the disinfectant cleaner used at the hospitals." Countless people also smelled this fragrance. The Lord Jesus was powerfully healing people from infectious disease. One precious older man was in severe ear pain. Liquid was draining from his ear. His face revealed only sadness and great discomfort. I prayed for his ear, and God dried up the infectious liquid. The next night he was lit up like a light bulb, totally healed and full of joy. The scent of the fragrance being emitted by the Holy Spirit is often an indicator of the work that God is accomplishing.

In Jerusalem while I was ministering at a prophetic conference, the fragrances of the Lord swept into the meeting with tremendous force. Fragrances of roses, lily of the valley, and other floral smells, along with myrrh and frankincense were so gloriously thick that hundreds of people were acutely aware of God's manifested presence. This lasted for several days. Because the meetings were being broadcast on live television, there were reports coming in from people around the world who smelled the same fragrances while watching the broadcast!

There have been countless times in meetings when the Lord's presence can be easily discerned because of His fragrance. During times of strong prayer, the unmistakable smell of frankincense can sometimes be manifest. The smell of roses comes often because Jesus is the Rose of Sharon, which is the only rose that doesn't have thorns. The potent smell of fresh grape juice, representing joy and the Holy Spirit, is often released.

When I am in the Spirit, the Lord allows me to actually smell the fragrance of Christ upon His people. There is a minister in India who lives a very holy life. We are friends and see each other from time to time. Once when I saw him, a whole year had passed since our last meeting. When we met, I noticed the most unusual fragrance emitting from him. Kelly was with me; she smelled the same fragrance when we greeted him. It was a heavenly fragrance that cannot be duplicated on the earth. You can't put spiritual attributes in a bottle, unless you become a bottle filled with His glory, as a sanctuary for the Lord.

> *Do you not know that you are God's sanctuary, and that the Spirit of God has His home within you?* (1 Corinthians 3:16 Weymouth).

The Lord has good taste. He likes nice things. He likes fine cologne, and He can craft a fragrance just for you. Once I was in a meeting, sitting next to another preacher. He had the most wonderful fragrance on. I asked him, "What are you wearing that smells so good?" He said, "I'm not wearing any cologne." I was detecting his spiritual fragrance. Later in the conference, I was sitting on the front row getting ready to speak. Suddenly that same fragrance from my preacher friend swept right over me. I looked at the person next to me and said, "Brother _____ is here." The person responded, "How do you know?" It was simple; his fragrance gave him away. I turned around just as this same brother in the Lord took a seat right behind me. Over the years, I've had people ask me, "What fragrance are you wearing?" They are detecting the spiritual qualities that should flow out of every believer. We all should be emitting the fragrance of Christ. It will manifest differently through each of us. When we come together as a corporate body, we have the ability to spiritually lift others, just as a bouquet of beautiful flowers will scent the air and make the atmosphere more pleasing.

The variety of fragrances can be vast because the Holy Spirit can speak one-on-one with a person through a unique fragrance that has a special meaning to that individual. These manifestations all glorify the Lord Jesus and invoke within us a deep desire to know Him more, and to walk with Him where the cassia is grown, in the high places where we are invited to dwell with our God.

The combined ingredients of the anointing oil represent to us the character and inner qualities that are found in the Lord Jesus Christ. When we allow the Holy Spirit to lead us in the path of spiritual development, we discover that the same attributes of the Lord Jesus will begin to be expressed through our life. This is the rich reward and deep satisfaction of knowing that we are progressively being conformed into His image. This change becomes noticeable not only within our hearts, but also to those around us as well. Once the holy anointing oil is prepared it is then poured out for service. As you yield to the workings of the Holy Spirit in your life, you will see a more consistent process of God working not just in you— but also through you to touch and minister to the lives of others. May the Lord make your life to be a type of fresh, fragrant, and holy oil that is applied to the needs that God has destined for you to flow into.

ENDNOTE

1. *Merriam-Webster's Collegiate Dictionary,* 11th ed., s.v. "Carnal."

CHAPTER TEN

Olive Oil: The Holy Spirit

In addition to the four spices we have studied so far, we also have the olive oil that served as the *carrier* for the spices. The oil used in the service of the tabernacle had to be the *first* oil of the olive. In today's language, we would say *extra virgin* olive oil, which is the oil that is squeezed out on the first press, thus rendering the purest and freshest oil possible. The oils that were used back in the Bible days contained fragrant oils from the spices that were available to them. If you were a guest in someone's house, they would serve you some fragrant olive oil upon your arrival from a long trip. You could then rub the oil into your tired and aching feet. You can imagine how good that must have felt if you had walked across rocks and hot sand and were barefoot or only had a thin pair of leather sandals.

They did not have lotions and creams available as we do today. The olive oil was used for refreshing, and because they put aromatic spices in it there would be an antiseptic effect that proved very useful. Today we can take a hot shower to clean up if we get dirty or sweaty. Back then, they did not have that luxury. The fragrant oils were used to diffuse body odor and to help heal cuts or infections. Olive oil was part of their culture of hospitality. It is also a biblical symbol of the Holy Spirit.[1] In reflection of all the ingredients for the holy anointing oil, I ask you to meditate on the fragrant spices used—liquid myrrh, sweet-smelling cinnamon, calamus, cassia—and be conscious of their prophetic attributes in your devotional life and your public witness. The Holy Spirit will empower you to serve God with joy and great effectiveness in your outreach to others.

One of my favorite passages involving the Holy Spirit is found in Acts 10.

> *While Peter was still speaking these words, the Holy Spirit **fell** upon all those who heard the word* (Acts 10:44).

Peter was preaching to those in the home of Cornelius. I love how the Holy Spirit divinely interrupted the preaching. The Spirit *fell* upon those in the meeting. That's one of those joys you need to experience in order to grasp its beauty. The same thing has happened to me before in meetings. Once I was speaking at a youth conference in the Himalayan Mountain region. I spent the day waiting on the Lord in prayer to seek a message from God that would bless the people. While in prayer, a certain Scripture kept coming to me from the Book of Isaiah.

It shall come to pass in that day that his burden will be taken away from your shoulder, and his yoke from your neck, and the yoke will be destroyed because of the anointing oil (Isaiah 10:27).

In my heart I sensed the Lord was going to remove burdens and destroy yokes in the evening meeting in which I was to minister. After a time of prayer, I decided to leave my hotel room and enjoy some sunshine and fresh air. I found a bench to sit on in a nice little garden area on the hotel grounds. As I was sitting on the bench relaxing, I looked up into the only tree on the hotel lawn, and I noticed something unusual hanging in the tree. It looked like an animal yoke. I thought, "That's strange. That looks like a yoke, but why would it be here, hanging high in a tree?" I decided to walk into the hotel lobby and ask the manager at the front desk. I said to him, "What is that hanging in the tree?" He smiled and replied with broken English, "Oxen yoke!" Since it appeared nobody had used it for years, I asked him if I could take it to the meeting and then bring it back when done. He allowed me to do so.

That night I stood on the stage and had a friend hold the yoke for the people to see. I began to teach from Isaiah 10:27, and the people were readily receiving the message. Suddenly, without any warning, the Holy Spirit *fell* upon the people. My translator was a very kind Nepalese brother. He has a master's degree in English and is very fluent in translating. Normally, he is quiet, reserved, and very calm and composed in his behavior. But when the Spirit fell, this dear man lost all control and began laughing hysterically. I tried to carry on, but after a few efforts I realized he was totally overwhelmed by the Spirit.

At the same time, a very godly woman sitting on the front row who was one of the ministers in charge of orchestrating the event fell to the floor and began weeping uncontrollably. A glorious fragrance of the Lord had burst over her, overwhelming her with God's love and mercy—she was simply undone as God touched areas in her heart that needed to be healed.

Simultaneously, the Spirit of God fell upon the young people. There were tears, shouts of joy, screams of deliverance, and about every other type of reaction you could imagine all going on at the same time. I began to minister to many of them with the laying on of hands. Others I couldn't reach because bodies were strewn everywhere. It looked like a spiritual bomb had gone off. In one last attempt to reach some that I couldn't get to, I took my neck-tie off from around my neck, laid my hands on it, prayed over it, and then threw it into the crowd. The young people caught it and passed it around. Many testified of the fragrance of beautiful flowers emanating from the tie. This lasted from eight o'clock in the evening until about midnight. As I walked back to my hotel, I could see men, women, and young adults staggering on the road as though drunk. Some people, including full-grown adults, had to be carried by others over a mile away to where they slept because of being so inebriated with the Spirit. Even as I lay in bed in my hotel room high up in the mountains, I could still hear the young people crying out to God until four o'clock in the morning. The minister who hosted the event said it was one of the most drunken services he had ever seen.

The Spirit of the Lord desires to work through us. We see clearly in Scripture that the Spirit of the Lord rested upon

Jesus during His earthly ministry. Isaiah the prophet speaks of the seven manifestations of the Holy Spirit that would rest upon the Lord.

> *The Spirit of the Lord shall rest upon Him, the Spirit of wisdom and understanding, the Spirit of counsel and might, the Spirit of knowledge and of the fear of the Lord* (Isaiah 11:2).

There are not seven Holy Spirits. There is only one Holy Spirit, yet He is displayed through these seven manifestations that rested upon Jesus. The Spirit of God can also rest upon the believer in order to anoint that person to function in his or her assigned calling. The anointing upon a person can be increased through obedience to God and time spent in the Word and prayer.

In Luke chapter 4 we read of the time when Jesus went and preached in the synagogue of His hometown of Nazareth. Jesus was handed the scroll of Isaiah and he deliberately found and read the text of Scripture that we identify as Isaiah 61:1, and the first part of verse 2. Jesus read to the people, saying, *"The Spirit of the Lord is upon Me"* (Luke 4:18). This famous portion of Scripture was prophetically speaking of the coming Messiah.

After reading those verses,

> *He closed the book, and gave it back to the attendant and sat down. And the eyes of all who were in the synagogue were fixed on Him* (Luke 4:20).

The story in Luke tells us that all the eyes of the people in the synagogue were fixed on Him. When reading this story, we can't help but be curious as to why the people's eyes were fixed on Him. What happened that caused the people to be so fixated?

When you study Jewish customs and traditions, you find an interesting practice that took place in Jesus' day, and can still be observed in some synagogues even today. The Jews reserve three special chairs in their synagogues, which are kept for three separate individuals. One chair is called the "Seat of Moses." That chair is for the minister or Rabbi to sit in. The second chair is called the "Seat of Elijah." It is for a guest minister or teacher to sit in. The third chair is reserved for the greatest guest of all, one that is expected to eventually arrive—it is for the Messiah. Well, after Jesus finished speaking it appears He sat down in the Messiah's chair! He actually sat in that reserved chair, and it caught all the attention of those in attendance.[2] The people in that meeting that day were all Jewish. When they saw Jesus "sit down," they instantly knew what that meant. That was a bold move for Jesus to make. That's why the people couldn't take their eyes off of Him. That prophetic act identified Him as the Messiah. Jesus spoke to those in the synagogue and said, *"Today this Scripture is fulfilled in your hearing"* (Luke 4:21). He basically told them, "That Scripture is talking about Me." Jesus knew He was the Anointed One.

The anointing that is upon you is for service. God anoints you with His Spirit to empower you to do the work He has called you to do. For example, the Lord has placed an anointing upon my life for miracles of healing. This gift, which is a special anointing He gave to me, has taken me around the world in the work of the ministry. When that anointing comes upon me and others release their faith to receive that anointing, the results are always the same—miracles! I've seen it happen in America and all over the world with creative miracles occurring and all types of diseases healed. Just as there is an anointing *upon*, there is also an anointing *within*.

> *But you have an anointing from the Holy One, and you know all things* (1 John 2:20).

> *But the anointing which you have received from Him **abides in you**, and you do not need that anyone teach you; but as the same anointing teaches you concerning all things, and is true, and is not a lie, and just as it has taught you, you will abide in Him* (1 John 2:27).

Notice we are told where the anointing abides: *"But the anointing which you have received from Him abides **in you**."* The anointing is within us. This anointing teaches us concerning all things. Some take this Scripture out of context and misuse it to imply that we do not need instructors or teachers. However, Jesus is the head of the Church, and He established the five ministry offices as gifts to the Church. The ministry office of the teacher is one of the five offices mentioned in Ephesians chapter 4. So, we need teachers. To reject the biblical ministry of the teacher is to reject a precious gift from God.

The anointing within you is for guidance and protection. It teaches you what is from God and what is not.

> *These things I have written to you concerning those who try to deceive you* (1 John 2:26).

The anointing within you protects you from deception, just as a virus software program protects your computer from malicious infections. When corrupt teaching is presented, the anointing within you goes off like an alarm. The anointing says, "Watch out; something is not right there!" When something is wrong, you have an uneasy feeling on the inside. When something is right, you should have a peaceful, velvety-smooth feeling on the inside.

The anointing *within* helps you to know all things. The more sensitive a person becomes to the anointing within, the more success they will have in making the right decisions in life. We should use our brain and utilize the best of our mental abilities. However, the anointing resides within your spirit, not within your physical brain. Yes, the anointing of God certainly affects the brain, which influences us to think godly thoughts. But some decisions we have to make in life go beyond the ability of one's brain to solve: Who to marry? Where to work? Where to go to church? What color should I paint the house? The answer to these types of questions should be measured through the anointing that resides within us.

Other questions such as, "Was the prophecy that person gave me from God, or not?" or, "How do I know if God has called me to the ministry?" The Holy Spirit will guide us through the anointing that God has placed within us. There's no need to be in the dark when it comes to knowing God's will and purpose. Let the anointing within you help settle the perplexing questions and choices you face. You can always trust the anointing of the Holy Spirit that abides within you to point you in the right direction.

The more developed you become in recognizing the inward anointing, the greater will be your ability to carry the glory of God. Understand that the anointing within you is what supports the potential anointing that can rest upon you. For example, some ministers have had a strong anointing upon them. This anointing initially came through God's grace in which He bestowed spiritual gifts through His own choice. The gifts and callings of God are irrevocable (see Rom. 11:29). These spiritual gifts were received by men and women through an act of God's grace. But some individuals have had major failures, with some falling from ministry and never fully recovering. How does a tragedy like this happen?

The reason a spiritual collapse takes place is because the inward anointing comprised of biblical morals, holy character, humility, and other spiritual attributes was deficient in that person's life. The inward anointing was not valued or developed, so such an individual could not support the weight of the anointing of God. We see this clearly in the life of Samson. What a unique and mighty anointing came upon him! The nation of Israel had never seen anything like it before. But we all know the unfortunate outcome of his life. It's how we finish that's important, not necessarily how we start out.

It is up to us to train ourselves to be diligent and instantly obedient to follow the inward anointing. By doing so, we will partake of the fruits of obedience that God so richly brings forth. The sacred anointing oil is a prophetic symbol of the Holy Spirit. Just as David spoke of in Psalm 92, we should all desire to be anointed with fresh oil.

But my horn You have exalted like a wild ox; I have been anointed with fresh oil (Psalm 92:10).

It's important for preachers to carry that fresh anointing upon their ministry. Years ago, I remember one particular minister who had a marvelous ministry. I could listen to him preach all day long. But over a period of time, something began to decline in his spiritual walk. Instead of fresh, anointed messages, he would simply retell old stories and repeat sermons that had been preached before. He had lost his edge. His prayer life was no longer vibrant, and it was reflected in his preaching. Eventually, his marriage also fell apart, and he went through a devastating divorce. When the anointing upon him was fresh, the devil couldn't touch him, but when he experienced international success and notoriety, he began to neglect the very principles and spiritual disciplines that God had used to establish him. We must be careful to honor the Holy Spirit and to stay in the anointing. A lifestyle of prayer should be an established practice from which we never drift and which we value and diligently protect, for our prayer life is literally the source of the anointing.

ENDNOTES

1. See http://bibletools.org/index.cfm/fuseaction/Topical. show/RTD/cgg/ID/1107/Oil-as-Symbol.htm.

2. http://www.liturgica.com/html/litEChLitJ. jsp?hostname=liturgica.

CHAPTER ELEVEN

How Prayer Influences the Anointing

While in prayer one day, the Lord revealed to me a secret found in the Book of Exodus chapter 30. I had been studying about the ingredients in the anointing oil, but often I felt drawn by the Lord to look across the page of my Bible and read about the ingredients used in preparing the holy incense. The Lord spoke to my heart and said, "The reason you are drawn to these two items simultaneously is because they are divinely connected, and serve a dual purpose together."

The ingredients for the anointing oil and for the incense are different, but yet they are both made from a group of closely related spices, and they are listed together in corresponding order in the same chapter. They are also made from four major ingredients. While the incense has seven ingredients, three of them are derived from cinnamon, so they are made from four primary sources. Their mutual correspondence can be seen through this fascinating verse, translated literally from the Hebrew language, in which King Solomon said:

> *Ointment and perfume* [qetoreth—incense] *delight the heart* (Proverbs 27:9a).

If we think of anointing oil as representing the anointing of the Holy Spirit, it may be useful to think of the fragrant incense as representing prayer. These two are placed in divine consecutive order because it is impossible to be anointed for ministry if there is not a vibrant prayer life. Prayer is what energizes the anointing. The anointing upon an individual can be increased through a sustained lifestyle consisting of quality time spent in daily prayer. Because of the importance that prayer plays in the role of the anointing, I felt it necessary to share in this chapter about the subject of prayer, as revealed through the incense that God instructed Moses to make.

> *And the Lord said to Moses: "Take sweet spices, stacte and onycha and galbanum, and pure frankincense with these sweet spices; there shall be equal amounts of each. You shall make of these an incense, a compound according to the art of the perfumer, salted, pure, and holy"* (Exodus 30:34-35).

The holy incense speaks to us of a life devoted to God in prayer. While the composition of the holy incense was a complex project requiring the utmost effort from highly skilled artisans, we can be comforted in knowing that the practice of effective prayer can be achieved by new believers as well as those who have been in the Church for decades. One of the greatest nuggets of truth I could share with anyone concerning prayer is "just go and pray." There are some things about prayer that we will be constantly learning, but the main thing is to act upon that which we already know. The best way to learn to pray is to just start praying. If you don't know how to pray, then the second best thing to do is get around someone who does. This is how God pulled me in closer to Him.

When I was in college, I met another student who would always get up early (5:45 A.M.) to go and pray by himself in the snack room in the dormitory in which we lived. His devotional life intrigued me greatly. One day I asked him if I could join him. He said, "Sure, I'll see you in the morning." To my great surprise, I actually got up and met with him. He went over to one corner of the snack room and kneeled down and prayed alone, and I went to the other corner in the room and prayed there. Every five minutes I would look over my shoulder to watch him and try to make sure I was "doing it right." That first morning I prayed for a whole 20 minutes. It may sound silly, but to me then it was an overwhelming experience. It was life changing. Over the next month, I worked my way up to being able to pray nonstop for 40 minutes. I'll tell you what, I thought I had reached the pinnacle of spirituality! But before long the semester ended, summer came, and when I returned to the dormitory for the next school year, my friend had moved somewhere else. I never regained my momentum until years later when I was filled with the Holy Spirit.

After being filled with the Holy Spirit in 1991 and speaking in tongues, the Lord led me to the teachings on prayer by Dr. David Yongii Cho, who pastors the world's largest church in Seoul, Korea. Immediately, my prayer life flourished, and it has been increasing ever since. Over a period of time, I was also exposed to the outstanding teachings on prayer by other men like Kenneth Hagin and Charles Finney. If your prayer life is flat and dull, you need to read and study anointed teachings on the subject of prayer to rekindle the fire. You simply cannot afford ever to let your prayer life fizzle.

Many of the wonderful personal experiences I have had with the Lord have all been based on time spent in prayer. People sometimes say, "But, Brother Steven, you are supposed to pray. You are a preacher." It is true that preachers should pray so that they can minister effectively, but I don't pray just because it simply prepares me to minister to others. I pray because I love the Lord. It's for my own personal joy and pleasure. Yes, I get messages out of my time spent with God that bless the people. But I don't necessarily go to the Father to get a message. I go to Him in prayer because there is nothing on this earth that is more satisfying, uplifting, or wonderful then just being with Him. There are other times, however, when I do go before God with requests and petitions that are on my heart.

> Be anxious for nothing, but in everything by prayer
> and supplication, with thanksgiving, let your requests
> be made known to God (Philippians 4:6).

It's out of the time that I spend with the Father in prayer that some of the most unusual experiences have happened to me. Toward the close of 2008, I went to the office to spend the night in prayer. After being in prayer for several hours, I felt as if my prayers had never gotten past the roof over my head. There was not enough anointing to lift a feather off the ground. I want to share this story with you to help you realize that we must pray in faith and not by feelings. That night there were absolutely no feelings. No goosebumps—no tangible anointing of any kind. As I pressed on in prayer, it seemed as if all my efforts to seek God were to no avail. Finally, I went over to my office desk and sat in my chair. I felt exhausted and physically drained. There was a total absence of God's presence. Leaning forward on my desk, I placed my head in my hands and made one final effort to *reach out* to God. With great exertion, I said, "Dear Father, would you please teach me about the apostolic ministry that you have for me?" As I spoke those words, I began to weep, because for several months I sensed the Lord wanted to speak to me about advancing in this calling, but I had not received any particular revelation regarding it.

Now, what I want to say next I want to describe as accurately as possible, so I'm choosing my words carefully in an effort to relate to you exactly what occurred. As I sat in my chair, the Lord Jesus Christ, the Head of the Church, the Resurrected Lamb of God, came into my office with an overwhelming presence. I did not see Him with my physical eyes. There have been times when I have seen the Lord with my physical eyes, but this time I did not physically see Him. But His presence, such as that of a king or prime minister, filled the room. Every trace of dryness was gone. I know exactly what the prophet Isaiah meant when he said:

In the year that King Uzziah died, I saw the Lord sitting on a throne, high and lifted up, and the train of His robe filled the temple (Isaiah 6:1).

Every square inch of my office that was previously flat and dry, was now completely filled with the glory of God. Immediately I got out of my chair and went to the front of my desk where the presence of God was strongly manifested. I knelt down on both knees. There was already a pen and notepad on my desk, so I reached over and grabbed them just before the Lord spoke. The Lord's voice came to me out of that holy presence that had filled the room. The communication was telepathic; it was not audible to my natural ear, but in my mind I distinctly heard Him speak to me.

He spoke and said, "I want to talk with you about your calling to the apostolic ministry." For the next 45 minutes, Jesus explained to me the role He has for me in this calling. The first ten minutes together we talked about the next group of nations He would be sending me to. The meaning of the word *apostle* is a "sent one." I've already been to quite a few nations. Some nations I have been to multiple times for ministry. But these were new doors that He was going to be opening for me. As we talked, I earnestly wrote down what He told me. Some of it I had to come back to after the vision ended and then write it down while it was still fresh so I wouldn't miss or forget anything He said.

After talking further, Jesus did something surprising. He reached back behind Himself and grabbed the edge of a purple curtain. He pulled back the curtain, and behind it I saw standing the most majestic-looking white horse I have ever seen. This horse was enormous, and it appeared to be about 15-feet tall. It was muscular and had the appearance of a Belgian Draft Horse. It was not a race horse, but rather a work horse that exhibited tremendous strength and power. The Lord said, "This is your angel in charge over your international travel needs. You will fly business class because you will go so often." As I looked at the horse, I knew it was an angel who had transformed himself to appear as a horse (see 2 Kings 6:17). The Lord spoke again, saying, "His name is Mysterion—he's also a historian." There was a distinct play on words as the Lord smiled and said, "The name of your angel is actually mentioned in My Word." Well, I've never been one to be shy. Can I tell you what I did next? I did the same thing you would probably do. I got up on that giant horse and sat on his back. As I did, I saw my wife and daughter appear in a picture behind my back, sitting with me on the horse.

After sitting there on Mysterion for a few moments, I dismounted from the horse, and the Lord continued talking with me further about my ministry. He said, "You will meet kings, queens, and governors, and other dignitaries so that you may pray for them. I will fill your schedule. I will raise your level." As we continued talking, He eventually concluded by saying, "I have need of you. I've placed My anointing in you and upon you to heal a sick and dying world. Go in the power of My Spirit! I have provided all you need to succeed. Go! I will speak to those of My own choosing to support you. For you will never lack or shrink back. Go now, and fulfill thy calling." As Jesus turned and began to walk away, He stopped at the edge of my office and turned His head toward me and said, "My television calling for you will not hinder your primary calling, which is to go and teach all nations." When He said those words, He then turned forward and walked right through the wall of my office and disappeared.

We need to learn to be persistent in prayer. I'm glad that on the night the Lord came that I didn't quit praying and go home just because I didn't *feel* something. Even though it was initially difficult to pray that evening, the Holy Spirit helped me not to give up. Several days after that vision, I was reading through my Bible looking for the name of the angel whom Jesus had assigned to my international travel needs. While reading through Colossians, I came across the following verses and did some research.

> *I now rejoice in my sufferings for you, and fill up in my flesh what is lacking in the afflictions of Christ, for the sake of His body, which is the church, of which I became a minister according to the stewardship from God which was given to me for you, to fulfill the word of God, the **mystery** which has been hidden from ages and from generations, but now has been revealed to His saints. To them God willed to make known what are the riches of the glory of this **mystery** among the Gentiles: which is Christ in you, the hope of glory* (Colossians 1:24-27).

Equipped with my *Vine's Expository Dictionary of New Testament Words,* I looked up the meaning of the word *mystery.* In the Greek language, it is the word *musterion* and refers to a "hidden thing, secret, or mystery."[1] Angels are sometimes given names that can be found in the Bible of places, events, or specific words. Here we see my angel mentioned in the Bible, just as Jesus told me. Recently I took my wife and daughter with me on another international ministry trip to Europe. This time it was a joy for us to fly business class on the German national airline, Lufthansa. The extra leg room and reclining seats are a tremendous help on long-haul flights. I believe when God gives us a specific promise, we must trust Him and exercise our faith and expect that God will bring it to pass. I'm also standing in faith for my own ministry jet so that I can travel further, faster, and more efficiently, and to more places not serviced by commercial airlines in the work of the Lord. My next step of faith is to transition from commercial airline business travel to general aviation business travel aboard our *own* jet. I believe this is what the Lord was fully implying when He spoke to me about going *business class.* This powerful ministry tool will be a tremendous assest in saving time and improving productivity. Recently I flew on a private jet to a meeting and landed at a small airport not serviced by any commercial airlines. To drive would have taken almost four hours. I flew out of my local airport in North Wilkesboro and flew straight to my destination. The total flight took thirteen minutes. The flight back also took thirteen minutes. To drive out and back would have taken over eight hours, as compared to twenty six minutes total with the jet. I've already picked out the name for my new jet, you may have guessed it – Mysterion.

It's important that whatever our calling is, whether it be ministry, business, or any honest endeavor, that we advance in that calling. For instance, the Lord recently revealed the importance to me of advancing in the apostolic calling. The three apostles that were closest to the Lord were Peter, James, and John.

> *Now after six days Jesus took Peter, James, and John his brother, led them up on a high mountain by themselves; and He was transfigured before them* (Matthew 17:1-2a).

Although there were 12 apostles, Jesus took only these three men up on the mountain with Him to be eyewitnesses of His transfiguration. But out of the three, John had the deepest spiritual walk. He was the one who leaned his head on the Lord's chest. God chose John to write the final book in the Bible, the Book of the Revelation of Jesus Christ.

The Lord revealed to me that in my own personal apostolic ministry I had progressed beyond the "Peter" level. The "Peter" level includes moving in the gift of special faith, working of miracles, and mighty signs and wonders. In my own ministry, I've seen all types of miracles and unusual signs and wonders. After 15 years of ministry, the Lord showed me that I am now currently in the "James" level. James was an apostle who could not be controlled by the fear of man. James called those in the Church who loved the world as being adulterers and adulteresses. The standard that James lived by was the Word, and he held to that standard whether it was popular or not. The Lord shared with me that if I was faithful and fervent then I would reach the final position, which is the "John" level. This is the highest apostolic level, and it is based on the love and light of God. Before the Lord returns, we will see the apostolic teachings of John become the *prime meat* of the end-time, overcoming, and victorious Church. John's writings, which are in the back of the Bible, correspond with a message vital for living at the close of the end of the present age.

Persistent prayer is vital in meeting the needs that stand before us. Jesus tells us in Luke chapter 18 that we should always pray and not lose heart. We live in a day of crisis situations where many of God's people have been overwhelmed with discouragement brought on by problems and perplexing situations. Failing to pray in such an hour will only lead to disillusion and inescapable stress. There is a place that can be attained through prayer where deliverance is brought forth and peace is sustained within the heart. God will answer our prayers, but we must be willing to bow our knees and pray. So many believers will do anything and everything under the sun except pray. But fervent heartfelt prayer will carry one over into the realm of God's miracle-working power.

In the parable of the unjust judge, Jesus reveals to us the determination and the unrelenting efforts of a widow woman who would not give up until she was righteously vindicated by the judge. This woman pushed the situation constantly before the judge. The judge was dealing with her case in the same way that tea is brewed in the South—slow and carefree. The judge was in no rush and had no personal interest in the woman's case. In his eyes, she was just another case number like all the others. However, the judge soon noticed the woman's tenacity and her unwillingness to take a softer approach. This woman meant business. She was on a mission, and she absolutely refused to be denied. In response to this woman's doggedness, the judge said within himself,

Though I do not fear God nor regard man, yet because this widow troubles me I will avenge her, lest by her continual coming she weary me (Luke 18:4-5).

Jesus uses this parable to teach us to be persistent in prayer. Jesus was not trying to identify God as an unrighteous judge, but rather as a God who responds to consistent, burning prayer. Our approach should not be to wear God out until He is so frustrated with us that He responds with an answer in disdain just to get rid of us. That's not the picture Jesus was trying to convey. Jesus uses this story as a parable to teach the value of strong, persistent prayer that is put forth until God moves as a result of our fervent petitions. This often involves praying more than just once, or longer than a few minutes. This type of praying engages us in a commitment that occupies our attention and priorities.

In my walk with the Lord I have discovered that this type of prayer is not only effective, but that it is *greatly effective*. It reminds us very distinctly of the similar and beautiful statement mentioned of the *great grace* that rested upon the early church.

And with great power the apostles gave witness to the resurrection of the Lord Jesus. And great grace was upon them all (Acts 4:33).

This is not just regular grace; this is identified as being called *great grace*. This is God's ability not only to answer prayer, but to do it in a way that is absolutely amazing. This type of praying must be revived in our lives. You don't have to wait on a revival. Start your own personal revival within your own life. The key to any revival that has ever happened or ever will happen is prayer. This can be accomplished individually for personal spiritual awakening, or it can be done corporately producing a firestorm of glorious results. The early church knew that prayer was the only way to sustain a move of God's Spirit. This *great grace* is coming again upon God's people to consume them with a genuine burden to pray until a divine release from Heaven is issued upon their behalf.

The ingredients used in the holy incense were stacte, onycha, galbanum, and pure frankincense. *Stacte* is another word for *myrrh*. The skilled perfume makers of Moses' day were anointed by God to create this complex fragrance that used myrrh as a *fixative*. A *fixative* is an oil that causes the fragrance of other oils to last longer, when they are mixed together.

Onycha is a powerful antiseptic that is derived from the resin of a tree that grows primarily in Indonesia. Some of the stories that I've read and studied regarding the ability of onycha to heal are simply remarkable. Deep cuts healing with no scars, chunks of flesh torn off in accidents growing back with brand-new flesh, and wounds healing with no pain or pus, are just many of the countless modern-day testimonies associated with onycha. Onycha has a strong antiseptic smell and has been used in hospitals for more than one hundred years. This smell is the fragrance most commonly associated with the "hospital smell" that you notice in hospitals. God truly put together a powerful combination of oil in the holy incense.

Galbanum is a potent evergreen smelling plant that is found in Northern India and Afghanistan. Galbanum, like frankincense and myrrh, is produced by cutting (wounding) the bark of the plant, which allows the resin to flow in the appearance of tears. It is related to the giant fennel plant with its large yellow, flowering heads.

Pure frankincense has a deep, woody aroma that is highly valued for its therapeutic uses, especially for bronchitis and asthma. Modern science has documented the tremendous anti-arthritic properties of frankincense. The active compounds are shown to inhibit joint inflammation and even alleviate depression and mood swings. Used for thousands of years, it is one of the most well-known oils in the world.

These oils were combined together in equal amounts, and then sweet spices were selected by the incense maker to mix in. The incense was then salted, and beaten to the proper consistency in a highly complex task that was carried out by a specific family within the priestly tribe. The exact procedures have been kept secret by this particular Jewish family for thousands of years now, protecting the holy incense from ever being used for pagan rituals, or any other purpose rather than its intended use.

There's no doubt in my mind that the holy incense kept the Aaronic priesthood free from many diseases. As the incense was burnt, it produced the effect of a powerful but wonderful smelling fumigant, in a process by which the molecules of the oils are released into the air by smoke. Breathing smoke is a very efficient way of absorbing the active ingredients in a plant. Of course, this can be beneficial or harmful, depending on what kind of smoke you are breathing.

Living in North Carolina, I am conscious of the effect of the tobacco industry because North Carolina leads the nation in product output.[2] As a guest speaker, I have often been tickled by how frequently pastors will inquire about my hotel needs by asking, "Do you need a smoking or non-smoking room?" Now that's a clear example of the kind of smoke that I **do not** want to inhale!

The ingredients used in the composition of the holy incense provide a natural barrier against germs and harmful bacteria. The incense that was burned in the Old Testament was a prophetic symbol of prayer. A strong prayer life establishes a protective barrier around your life that also blocks access to worry, stress, sickness, and disease. Back in the Old Testament days, most of the people had no understanding of the microscopic world of germs, which are so small they can only be seen through some means of amplification. The smoke from the incense had an aromatic quality to it that was conducive to hindering the spread of harmful germs. We see an example of this in the Book of Numbers chapter 16, when Moses told Aaron to take a censor with fire and incense on it, and then go out to stop a plague that had already killed over 14,000 people. The smoke from the incense acted as a natural fumigant that killed airborne bacteria.

I think we all need to inhale as much of God's *holy smoke* as possible. Spiritual germs and unclean "critters" will have to vacate the premises when God's holy smoke pervades our atmosphere. Regular fumigations of God's holy smoke—His Holy Presence—are needful to eradicate unclean thoughts, impure motives, and other contaminated "mental microbes." Prayer, fervent prayer, will produce the same cleansing, sanitizing results as the holy incense did in the days of old. We need to burn more holy incense to God. We need to order our lives so that prayer is not an option, but a necessity to which lesser priorities must take a back seat. We must stay on our knees until there is a *saturation* of God's holy smoke that is inhaled by our inner man, until our thoughts are no longer our thoughts, but are derived from the Holy of Holies.

We also see with the holy incense that God told Moses not to make any of it for himself. If anyone tried to make it for themselves to enjoy its fragrance, they were to be cut off from the people. The rabbis teach that the incense that was compounded weighed 368 maneh (measures). This relates to the need for us to pray daily, as there was one measure used each day, half in the morning and half in the evening. The other three measures were those that the High Priest would bring into the Holy of Holies as a double handful on Yom Kippur. The holy incense was holy because it represented the prayers of the saints.

> *Now when He had taken the scroll, the four living creatures and the twenty-four elders fell down before the Lamb, each having a harp, and golden bowls full of incense, which are the prayers of the saints* (Revelation 5:8).

Isaiah spoke of the day when the Gentile nations would turn to the Lord.

> *They shall bring gold and incense* (Isaiah 60:6).

The nations of the world are ripe for a spiritual harvest of souls. As the multitudes find salvation in Jesus, we will see the incense (prayer) rise to the Father in thanksgiving for having been told of the good news of salvation through Jesus Christ.

The holy incense was the fragrance of God as revealed in the Old Covenant. You could say it was God's *signature scent.* A *signature scent* is a fragrance that is custom made to uniquely fit and showcase an individual's personality, taste, and style. Dr. Richard Axel, MD, won the Nobel Prize in Physiology or Medicine in 2004 for his research on the olfactory (scent) system. Dr. Axel revealed that 5 percent of our genetic makeup is composed of our sense of smell, which is a higher makeup than the physical senses of vision and hearing. Perhaps this is why God places such a high priority on the premium ingredients used to make the holy incense. As you fully commit your heart to a lifestyle devoted to prayer, I believe that God will place His own signature scent upon your life, that of His Son, Jesus.

> *For we are to God the fragrance of Christ...*(2 Corinthians 2:15a).

ENDNOTES

1. See "musterion"; http://www.studylight.org/lex/grk/view.cgi?number=3466.

2. See http://www.agr.state.nc.us/markets/commodit/horticul/tobacco/.

Chapter Twelve

The Power to Live Your Dream

We all have distinct dreams to walk out on this earth. There are certain deposits that God makes within our spiritual DNA that cause us to go certain directions in life. It's like a select group of birds that migrate and inherently know where to go when they have never been there before. God put within them the *knowing* of what they were created to do. When you become born again through the precious blood of the Lord Jesus, your identity in Christ becomes clear, and your purpose in life begins to unfold. The Heavenly Father has sent the Holy Spirit to the earth, and we have the angels to assist us. The Lord Jesus has also given us the authority to use His name and to bind and loose on the earth. We have been given the "goods" to get the job done, and we must pursue our God-given calling.

The enemy of your soul does not want you to fulfill your God-given dream. As you step out in faith, you can be sure that the devil will be there to throw up all sorts of barriers and hindrances to discourage you. This is where you must use your faith in God's Word and stand your ground to enforce the enemy's defeat. Jesus defeated the devil and every foe of darkness at Calvary through His death, burial, and triumphant resurrection. He is gloriously enthroned at the right hand of God. Now Jesus expects us to *go forth* and further His Kingdom. The Lord's Kingdom is *within* the heart of man. The day is soon approaching in which Jesus will literally rule physically with an earthly kingdom. The earthly kingdom will take place during the 1,000-year reign of the Lord. We are to occupy till He comes. We see this expressed through a parable that Jesus taught concerning His Kingdom.

> *And He called His ten servants, and delivered them ten pounds, and said unto them, "**Occupy** until I come"* (Luke 19:13 KJV).

The word *occupy* in the Bible is a word expressing a military and business aspect. It means to "take possession of a strategic position." It also means to "keep busy" or "to engage."[1] Your God-given dream should be based upon an underlying purpose of occupying until He comes. The Lord desires for us to occupy every place of authority in the financial market, the media, the political arena, the medical system, and every other system that has the ability to influence people. This is not an option; this is a mandate. We are to do this *until* He comes. Our goals, dreams, and visions should be linked to this cause.

Along the path to the fulfillment of your dream you are sure to encounter the devil's resistance, for he will attempt to stop or impede your progress when it pertains to furthering God's Kingdom. The devil will not hinder the progress of a beer company or a pornographic print shop. Those types of industries further *his kingdom,* so they operate smoothly upon the anti-anointing of a world system that is already passing away. In contrast, we are like the salmon that have to swim upstream against the current to reach their destination. The believer who desires to further God's Kingdom has to do it in a world of spiritual darkness where the devil has influence and leverage.

> *The god of this present age has blinded their unbelieving minds so as to shut out the sunshine of the Good News of the glory of the Christ, who is the image of God* (2 Corinthians 4:4 Weymouth).

This is why the Church needs to know how to deal with the devil. Satan is the "god" of this world. The Church has to use their authority over him in order to advance God's Kingdom. The devil has authority over the unbeliever, but he has no authority over a believer. I know some Christians think and teach that the devil can just walk into your life and do anything he wants to, but the only way the devil can gain authority over a believer *is if it is given to him,* whether knowingly or done through ignorance.

Think about your home, for instance. If you went to work and left your front door wide open, all the windows up and unlocked, the back door open, and the door to your safe vault in your home open, wouldn't it be possible for a thief to seek access at *your particular home*? The devil (who is a thief) is always looking for access. If you have a wealthy home, he will especially look to break into that home and steal the valuables. If a person has an anointing or special calling upon his life (spiritual wealth), satan will seek specifically to break into that person's life and destroy him. Shut the door on disobedience and turn on the alarm system of your faith. Deny him access into your life. He doesn't need a wide-open door; just a crack could be enough.

Willful disobedience to God and His Word gives the devil legal right to gain entry into the life of a believer. The devil is so cruel and full of hatred that often when he gains access he will destroy mercilessly. Years back I worked in a corporation where there was much immorality around me. This was not shocking because sinners only do what they know to do, which is to sin. One man in senior management was always very kind to me, and he was a born-again Christian. He was married to a very nice Christian woman and had two wonderful children. However, I knew personally that this man fell into regular sin with an unsaved woman at work. They committed adultery together on a regular basis. This was, of course, hidden from public knowledge, but I became aware and never told a soul.

One day this man's oldest son, who was in his early teens, was at school walking around the playground having fun with the other children, when he suddenly fell down dead from an inexplicable brain aneurism. People were shocked by this tragedy. The church did a beautiful job of supporting the family and comforting them. It was, however, disturbing to hear all the well-meaning statements such as, "God took your son home early because He needed him on the other side." The truth is that the devil gained access into that family through the father's great act of disobedience. Those believers who knew this man could not understand how a young boy could suddenly die with no apparent explanation.

I believe when we get to Heaven there will be many mysteries unraveled, and saints will be very surprised when they find out the real truth behind the cause of certain events. This doesn't mean we should view people with suspicion with regard to unexplainable tragedy. But we should be spiritually mature enough to realize that if something went wrong, *it wasn't God's fault*. We should be willing to acknowledge that it could be possible that we may have overlooked something.

God is very kind, merciful, and loving. When we break his commandments we hurt ourselves and potentially others as well. The laws of God's kingdom are for our safety and protection. David felt the sting and anguish of his adultery with Bathsheba and murder of her husband. God forgave David of his sin, but the enemy had already gotten in. The child conceived through David and Bathsheba died seven days after birth. The Bible says that David pleaded with God for the child. I have no doubt that David must have said, "Lord, let me die. The baby is innocent. Take my life instead. I am the one who did wrong." Even though David pleaded with all his heart, the child still died. The enemy had a legal right to kill the child because David, the child's father who had the authoritative covering over the child, opened the door to the destroyer. I want you to know the devil has no conscience. If you let him in, you can have a real mess on your hands. Be careful! Do not play around with sin.

Often, the devil works through people. These people can be unbelievers, and even at times Spirit-filled tongue-talking believers who may act unknowingly to do the devil's will. A believer and an unbeliever can yield to the devil if they choose to. Often, a believer will do so in ignorance, or perhaps unconsciously, by not being aware of their error. And it is very much possible that a believer can intentionally do something wrong while having full knowledge of it.

Because the devil attempts and sometimes succeeds in gaining access to work through people, we have to be careful that we do not try to deal with people in a natural way when the source of the problem is spiritual. That doesn't mean there aren't times when we have to deal with people in the natural. But I'm focusing now on dealing with problems that are spiritual, and the evil spirit working in the invisible realm that is causing the problem must be dealt with.

If you try to deal with people in the natural who are being influenced by evil spirits, you will not have very good success. Actually, you might even make things worse. When a person is under the influence of an evil spirit, it does not do much good to reason or analytically explain why their actions are wrong. Presently, this nation has opened the door over a period of time that has allowed multitudes of deceiving spirits to occupy this land. People who are under the influence of these deceptive spirits cannot be persuaded to change through good counsel nor can they be won over by argumentative debating. They cannot see the truth because they are *spiritually blinded*.

These deceptive spirits have gained access into this country because the majority of the Church allowed it. This is because much of the Church herself has been religiously busy but has failed to live a lifestyle of prayer. Now, the issue is no longer the nation being divided between conservative and liberal, but the mainstream Church in America becoming divided. Many church leaders and members today are embracing beliefs borrowed from the destroyed cities of Sodom and Gomorrah. This is because there are evil spirits of deception that are influencing the thought life of men and women.

The debates today between liberals and conservatives remind me very much of the debates between atheists and creationists. An atheist will express his views as to why he does not believe in God. The creationist will refute every question and then overwhelmingly demonstrate that the universe in which we live shows intelligent design and that it must have been made by a Creator. Despite the inescapable conclusion, the atheist will not change his beliefs. He is *spiritually* blind and cannot be set free merely through a verbal debate.

In contrast, the liberal expresses why he has no moral standards and insists that he should be allowed to do anything he wants, as long as it "doesn't hurt anyone else." The informed conservative skillfully shows the foolishness of such thoughts and explains how the fabric of society is held together by law, order, and godly principles. Despite another lopsided case of irrefutable evidence, the liberal still holds to his faulty belief system. This takes place because of the unseen realm where evil spirits suggest thought patterns that are contrary to the will of God.

This is why it is so critical to put the Word of God into the hearts of believers, particularly baby Christians who have just been saved. The Word of God will renew our minds and enable us to see clearly and truthfully. I believe a great wind of God's Spirit is about to blow upon this nation and clear the spiritual fog away from multitudes who have been in deception. Along with the wind of God's Spirit will come forth powerful preaching and teaching that will be presented with a greater level of authority than what we have become accustomed to. Many of the hardest hearts will be cut low by the Sword of the Lord.

We must exercise our spiritual authority to bind the plans of the enemy. We cannot exercise authority over a person's will. Each person has his or her own free will, and not even God will override a person's free will and choice. But we can exercise authority over the forces of evil that would try to work through people who block and hinder the will of God. Whenever there is something unusual that is causing the work of God to be hindered or delayed, the evil spirit that is causing that problem needs to be bound. The outward problem may be seen as being caused by a person, but the spirit operating through that person can be bound. To bind the evil spirit just say, "You foul spirit that is working through this person, I command you to stop and discontinue all your strategies and efforts in the Name of Jesus." It is up to us to exercise and use the authority Jesus has given us.

Many believers mistakenly think Jesus will take care of the devil for them. They sit back and relax thinking that "God is on the throne; He will take care of it." We need to understand that Jesus has *already* taken care of the devil for us at Calvary through His death, burial, and triumphant resurrection. It is up to us to stand our ground and let the Lord Jesus rule and reign through us. We have been seated with Christ in the heavenly realms through our being united in Him (see Eph. 2:6). Jesus delegated His authority to the Church to enforce the defeat of the enemy and to further the holy Kingdom of God. Don't just sit back and let the devil run rampant in your thought life, finances, physical body, or the sphere of life in which you have authority. Resist the devil; use the authority that Jesus has *already* given to you, and the enemy will flee from you.

The devil and evil spirits will try and block your God-given dream from being fulfilled. We are not going to become devil conscious and overemphasize his realm, but we do want to understand our authority over the kingdom of darkness that we might effectively overcome every opposition we may face. Not every problem, sickness, or disease is related to an evil spirit, but many of these cases are. The Holy Spirit is here to help us effectively navigate our way through every challenge we face. I'd like to share with you a few ways the Holy Spirit has helped me to minister to those who are influenced by evil spirits.

> *And behold, there was a woman who had a **spirit of infirmity** eighteen years, and was bent over and could in no way raise herself up* (Luke 13:11).

Notice that this woman suffered from a *physical* condition that had its roots connected to a *spiritual* condition. Over ten years ago I prayed for a woman in her late twenties who had a similar *physical* condition. She was bent over at a 90-degree angle with her face forced to look down at the ground. Her back was in terrible pain, and it took great effort to lift her head up to see what was in front of her. When I laid my hand on her back, she was instantly healed as she rose straight up from her previous position. She let out a big gasp of relief as she stood tall and free. It has been years now, and she has been healed ever since. However, the woman in the above verse had a physical condition that was caused by a *spirit of infirmity*. Not all sickness is caused by a spirit of infirmity. The woman I prayed for had a major degenerative back problem that was only a physical condition. If the case involves a spirit of infirmity, then often the spirit needs to be recognized and dealt with in order to minister effectively. This is because the spirit of infirmity is there to enforce the sickness, so the spirit must be made to leave for the healing to come forth.

> But when Jesus saw her, He called her to Him and said to her, "Woman, you are loosed from your infirmity." He laid His hands on her, and immediately she was made straight, and glorified God (Luke 13:12-13).

Jesus was made aware by the Holy Spirit that the woman was bound with a spirit of infirmity. How can we tell if the condition is just physical or if there is an evil spirit involved? The answer is that we have to rely on the Holy Spirit to guide us. I have discovered over the years that when the power of God comes into the proximity of evil there is a reaction. Because of ministering in many meetings, I have also experienced reactions that occur when encountering God's great glory. Sometimes people fall, shake, roll, vibrate, and display many other side effects. This is not necessarily a manifestation of the Spirit, but rather, a physical reaction of coming into contact or close proximity with God's Spirit.

About a year ago, I was ministering in a well-known Spirit-filled church in Southern California. After I preached a message, I then moved into ministering to the people prophetically. The Spirit of the Lord impressed me to call up a man who had a strong prophetic ministry that I might prophesy to him. As he came up, he got within seven feet of me, and he bumped right into my personal angel! A current of electricity went all through his body, and a look of such glory and awe came upon his face that he was completely immobilized. Endeavoring to help, I stepped forward and reached out to steady him. When I did my left arm brushed up against the angel, and I felt the soft, luxurious robe that he wore. Upon contact all the hair on my body stood straight up! It was absolutely electrifying and was an awesome rush of energy. The other minister was still numb to the physical world even several hours after the meeting. The message that I had preached that day was called, "How to Have a Visitation." Well, that dear brother walked right into a visitation!

On the other end of the spectrum, I've also had experiences of observing evil spirits being driven out by the Holy Spirit. In one instance about 15 years ago, I was talking with a Christian woman openly in the church parking lot after the morning service was over. She told me with deep sorrow of her husband's cruelness to her, as well as describing a severe spinal problem that caused excruciating pain. She seemed to have a heavy, dark cloud over her, and she suffered from chronic depression. Her weight had dropped to a dangerous level, and she was just skin and bone. After she described her condition, I suggested that we just sing a song of worship to the Lord, because He is bigger than any problem we could ever face.

As we sang a simple song of worship to the Lord, we suddenly felt the Holy Spirit come upon both of us in a mighty way. Recognizing the Lord's presence, we began to sing with all of our hearts the praises of God, extolling the Name of Jesus. As we did, she suddenly released the loudest, most gruesome burp I've ever heard. Instantly, I saw into the realm of the spirit, and I watched as an evil spirit of death crawled up out of her body and exited out through her mouth. As it left the woman's body, all the hair on the back of my neck stood up as it went right past me as it left the parking lot. There was a strong evil presence that surrounded that unclean spirit as it went by me. The woman then collapsed and fell forward onto the hood of her car. She lay there for about two minutes before slowly raising herself up. When she stood up, joy and light were shining upon her face. The dark cloud over her was gone, the spirit of death had been driven out of her, and in the process God mightily baptized her in the Holy Spirit. She then opened her mouth and prophesied powerfully about the greatness of God for over 20 minutes. She was completely healed of her back problem and totally set free from the demonic oppression. A few days later when I saw her I asked her if she remembered that outrageous burp. She had absolutely no knowledge that she had done that. She went on later in her life to enter the ministry and became an anointed teacher of God's Word.

These examples help us understand the clash that takes place in the spirit realm when two opposing kingdoms collide. Sometimes there is a reaction; other times there may be no outward manifestation, but the anointing still gets the job done. The Holy Spirit desires that we be sensitive to His leadings so that we can be effective in the Lord's work. I'm mindful of some of the ministers that ministered during the 1950s Healing Revival. Reverend Kenneth Hagin explained that when he ministered to the sick through the laying on of hands he could tell if there was an evil spirit present by placing one hand on each side of the person's body. Fire would jump from his one hand to the other hand if an evil spirit was causing the affliction. If the fire did not jump from hand to hand, then it was a case needing healing only.[2]

A similar anointing occurred in the healing ministry of Prophet William Branham. The sick person would place his or her right hand in Brother Branham's left hand. If the sickness or disease was caused by an evil spirit, then Brother Branham would feel a vibration in his own hand similar to an electric current. His left hand would also swell and turn various shades of color, depending on the disease. After he would cast the spirit out, his hand would return to normal, although his wrist watch would often stop due to the strong flow of power. William Branham endeavored to explain these manifestations in a letter he wrote to C. Parker Thomas.[3]

In my ministry, I am able to tell when a spirit of infirmity is causing a sickness in a person. This takes place by the Holy Spirit revealing supernatural information to me through the gift of discerning of spirits. I can know the source of the sickness when I am in the Spirit. Sometimes people ask me to minister to them when I am not in the Spirit. They'll catch me at a restaurant or call me at an odd time when I am relaxing or asleep. Unless I'm able to get in the Spirit, I cannot know certain things because I'm only human. The Holy Spirit has to help me. Now I can always pray the prayer of faith for a person and believe for a miracle, but it's different when ministering under the anointing.

Dealing effectively with evil spirits is not just for ministers. Resistance can come to any believer who strives to serve the Lord. These are principles that apply not just to healing, but also to your finances. For example, God has a good plan for your finances. The Lord wants you to have a full supply so that your needs are met and you have an abundance to bless others and further His Kingdom through tithes and offerings. Just as there are spirits of infirmity that try to hold people in sickness, there are also evil spirits that try to hold back financial increase.

As a reminder, we are not trying to focus on the devil, but there are times when the Holy Spirit can reveal to us spiritual resistance from the enemy that may need to be addressed accordingly. Failing to do so could cause delay or stop up a blessing that is intended by God to reach you. Some would say that if it is God's will, then it will happen regardless of what we do. But we have to pray, use our faith, and work hard to see God's will accomplished.

As my wife and I labored together in the ministry, we saw a pattern over the years of how the Lord continually increased our finances. When we started out, there was nowhere to go but up. The more we sacrificed and put God's Kingdom first, the more we saw the Lord bless us in all areas of our lives. However, even after quite a few years in the ministry, Kelly and I both were cognizant that we had never broken past a certain level in our finances. There was a barrier of a certain number that we would often receive, but never did we get an offering larger than this amount. The fact that we did receive this certain amount in many of our meetings told us that there was a wall of resistance that we needed to break through. Our reason for not going beyond this wall was not due to a lack of sowing seed. We had consistently given sacrificially. But our giving was not producing the type of harvest we should have been reaping.

One day we had our corporate prayer meeting at our ministry office to lift up the needs of the ministry. What took place next was completely unexpected. As we were praying, suddenly the Lord showed me a vision in the spirit realm of a river that at a certain place had a log jam that had blocked up the flow of water. Because the logs were all jammed together in bottleneck configuration, only a small amount of water was getting through. The log jam was a description of our financial situation. An evil spirit was hindering and holding back our rightful harvest. The vision ended as others around me were still corporately praying. Kelly was in her office getting ready to join the prayer meeting. When the vision ended, I jumped up, went to her office, and told her what I just saw. Together we then went and told the other intercessors what the Lord showed me. With this knowledge, we began to pray and bind the hindering spirit that was working to hold back finances that God wanted to flow into this ministry. Because of this information that the Lord showed me, coupled with the fact that an anointing was upon me, I bound that foul spirit and commanded it to cease and stop all of its actions, in the Name of Jesus Christ. I want you to know, with God as my witness, that two days later the Lord sent a person to my ministry office, and I was handed the largest financial gift that the ministry had ever received! It was as if the Lord took a keg of gunpowder and blew that log jam into smithereens! The river has been flowing fine ever since.

Don't let anything hold you back from fulfilling your God-given dream. You have the power. You have the authority. Jesus has given you the arsenal of Heaven to get the job done. Exercise your authority. Don't depend on someone else to do it for you. With God on your side and your faith on fire, you are certain to go from victory to victory. As you do, others will be inspired to live their dream too.

Endnotes

1. Merriam-Webster's Collegiate Dictionary, 11th ed., s.v. "Occupy."

2. Kenneth Hagin, *I Believe in Visions* (Tulsa, OK: Faith Library Publications, 1984), 51.

3. See http://wmb1.com/de/~diego/Specials/CPARKER_ Letter_from_William_Branham.shtml.

CHAPTER THIRTEEN

Closing Thoughts and Prayer of Impartation

In summation of the teachings shared in this book, I want to conclude by encouraging you to let God place a fresh anointing of His Spirit upon your life that you may be boldly empowered to fulfill all that God has called you to do.

I also want to conclude this book by stressing the importance of finding the gifting that God has given you and developing it to its fullest potential. It is wise to do this, for the area in which God has anointed you is the key source to your prosperity. When I mention prosperity, please do not limit this to only financial prosperity. God wants you to prosper spiritually by having a very close walk with Him. He wants your mind to prosper and for you to be brilliant, sharp, and knowledgeable in your skill. The Lord desires for your body to be in health so that you can enjoy life and fulfill the assignment upon your life. Without your body being healthy you would be limited as to what you could potentially accomplish.

As you allow God to freshly anoint you and thus continue to increase in the anointing, don't be surprised where the anointing of God's Spirit may take you.

A man's gift makes room for him, and brings him before great men (Proverbs 18:16).

Your gift—your anointing—has the potential to bring you before leaders, kings, presidents, and other dignitaries and people of influence. The anointing of God upon my life lifted me from the despair of living out of a cardboard box and eating out of dumpsters to now traveling throughout the earth ministering the Gospel message to multitudes of people through television and through personal ministry.

In my earlier years I could not identify God's purpose for my life. I drifted through life working many different jobs and was never happy with any of them. Due to this frustration, during my early twenties I took a "work placement" test that was used to identify which line of work a person would most likely be successful at. The test was administered to me by a kind lady who had a master's degree in psychology. With confidence, she told me, "Steven, after this test we will be able to know exactly which job is best for you." The test took several hours for me to complete. It had hundreds of questions, and I tried to answer each one as accurately as possible. Once I was finished, I turned it in and came back two days later to be informed of the results.

Upon returning, I sat down with the psychologist and she said, "Steven, your score is unlike any that I have seen before. You scored in the less than one percentile category." I said, "Well, what does that mean?" She replied, "It means that 99.9 percent of the jobs are unsuitable for you." By the age of 26, I had already worked 83 different jobs.

Looking back with hindsight, I can now clearly see that God was regularly dropping major hints to me about my specific gifting. As a senior in high school, the pastor of my local church stopped me in the foyer at the conclusion of a Sunday morning service on my way out. He said, "Steven, have you ever thought about being a preacher?" He never said that to any other young person. Over the next ten years, these types of statements began to escalate toward me through encouraging words, prophetic utterances, and other point-blank hints that helped me finally slip into my anointing, which is that of a preacher of the Gospel. Once I began working toward my set calling, there was a tremendous progression in my life in relation to understanding my purpose and experiencing on-going accomplishments.

Sometimes others around us can see more clearly about God's anointing upon our lives than what we may see. We may not see because of inherit deficiencies, such as a feeling of being unworthy or a low sense of self-esteem. Often there may be a lack of spiritual insight that produces an inability to discern God's will. I would encourage you that if you are getting the same encouraging word over and over again from multiple sources to certainly pray and consider what is being said. Your gift will make room for you, even if it initially may only be in its developmental stages. If you are already progressing in your respected area of anointing then allow God to empower you to go to the "next level." There is always room for more of the increased anointing of God.

Are you now ready to pray for God to anoint you with the fresh oil of His Holy Spirit? Please kneel down and pray this prayer to God.

"Dear Heavenly Father,

In the name of Jesus, I ask that the anointing that you have given me be fully identified in my life, along with its purpose and application. I ask for a special measure of your Spirit to rest upon me, to empower me to fulfill all that you have destined for me to accomplish. Heavenly Father, I ask that you anoint me to stand at the forefront of my respected calling. I commit to give you all the credit and glory for every blessing that you accomplish through my life. I pledge to remain humble in your sight, and to resist pride and all forms of arrogance and elitism. Strengthen me, Father, to apply myself to the fullest extent, to work earnestly, and to increase in the knowledge of You and Your ways, that my gifting may be developed to its fullest potential. Oh Lord God, place your mighty anointing of your Spirit upon my life—right now—and to you be all the praise and glory, forever and ever. Amen."

Now receive from God, as His Holy Spirit ministers to you now.

Prayer of Salvation and Holy Spirit Baptism

Perhaps you came across this book and have not yet had the opportunity to personally receive Jesus Christ as Savior and Lord. I would like to invite you to open your heart to Him now. Please read the following verses from the Bible out loud. When you read Bible verses out loud so that your physical ears can hear the Word of God, it allows faith to enter into your heart:

> *And it shall come to pass that whoever calls on the name of the Lord shall be saved* (Acts 2:21).

> *That if you confess with your mouth the Lord Jesus and believe in your heart that God has raised Him* [Jesus] *from the dead, you will be saved* (Romans 10:9).

> *And do not be drunk with wine, in which is dissipation; but be filled with the Spirit* (Ephesians 5:18).

> *And they were all filled with the Holy Spirit and began*

to speak with other tongues, as the Spirit gave them utterance (Acts 2:4).

Now that you have read how you may be saved, you can obey the Word of God and make your life right with God. Simply pray the following prayer from your heart, and Jesus will give you His eternal life.

"Dear Lord Jesus, I confess that You are the Son of God. I believe that You were raised from the dead and are alive forevermore. Please come into my heart and forgive me of all my sins. I turn away from all sin, and I give my life completely to You. Please fill me with Your precious Holy Spirit so that I may speak in tongues and worship You all the days of my life. Thank You, Jesus, for saving me and for filling me with Your Holy Spirit. I love You!"

Now lift your hands and begin to praise God for saving you. Open your mouth and begin to speak in the new heavenly language that the Holy Spirit has given you. Let the new words and syllables come forth, not your own language, but the language the Holy Spirit gives you. Don't be concerned about how it sounds. It might not make sense to your mind, but it is your spirit communicating with God, and God understands everything you are speaking.

Praise the Lord! You are now a Spirit-filled Christian on your way to Heaven. Every day speak in tongues to glorify God and to strengthen yourself. You will be refreshed as you do.

Now that you belong to Jesus, ask your Heavenly Father to help you find a church home so that you can grow spiritually and continue your walk with God. The Holy Spirit will lead you as you search for the Christian church that God wants you to be a part of. Look for a church where you can sense the love of God and where people take a genuine interest in you. Seek out a church that believes the whole Bible and preaches it without compromise. And always remember *that Jesus loves you.*

Ministry Partner Information

We would like to share with you a sincere and open invitation to partner with the life-changing ministry of Steven Brooks International. With the support of our precious Ministry Partners, Steven and Kelly are empowered to reach further into the nations of the world with God's Word and His healing touch. Working together we can experience a greater impact for the fulfillment of the Great Commission. With a world population approaching the staggering number of seven billion souls, the need has never been greater for anointed biblical teaching coupled with genuine manifestations of God's power to strengthen the Church.

Steven's life is dedicated toward the apostolic cause of ministering the bread of life to hungry souls around the world. Without the help of dedicated Ministry Partners, the great outreaches of this ministry would not be possible. The help of each Ministry Partner is vital. Whether the support is large or the widow's last two pennies, every bit helps in this worldwide outreach. With your prayers and generous financial support, we are endeavoring to go through the unprecedented doors of opportunity that the Lord is opening for this ministry.

Steven and Kelly absolutely treasure their Ministry Partners. Each Ministry Partner is viewed as a special gift from God and is highly valued. Steven and Kelly believe in covenant relationships and understand the emphasis and blessing that God places upon such divine connections. In this end-time hour God is joining those with like hearts to stand together in this sacred work. Thank you for prayerfully considering becoming a Ministry Partner. We encourage you to take the step and join this exciting and rewarding journey with us. Together we can make an eternal difference in the lives of precious souls, enabling us to have an expectancy to hear the Lord's voice on that blessed day, saying, "Well done, thou good and faithful servant."

As a Ministry Partner, your undertaking is to pray for Steven, his family, and his ministry on a regular basis and support his ministry with a monthly financial contribution.

As a Ministry Partner, you will receive the following benefits:

- Impartation that is upon Steven's life to be upon you to help you accomplish what God has called you to do

- Consistent prayer for you by Brother Steven

- Monthly Ministry Partner newsletter to build your faith and feed your spirit

- Mutual faith in God for His best return on all your giving

- Eternal share in the heavenly rewards obtained through this ministry

---

Become a Ministry Partner today!

Name _____

Address _____

Phone Number _____

E-mail Address _____

_____ Yes, Brother Steven. I join with you in Ministry Partnership, and I (we) stand with you as you continue to preach the Gospel to all the earth and usher in the return of the Lord Jesus Christ.

You may also become a Ministry Partner by registering at our online Web site at
www.stevenbrooks.org.

Click on the "Partner" link to sign up.

About the Author

The ministry of Steven and Kelly Brooks continues to reach multitudes of souls around the world. Steven is widely known for his ability to teach God's Word in a clear and understandable way to new believers as well as to those who have been in the faith for decades. He walks in a remarkable gift of *working of miracles*, and divine healing is a trademark of his ministry. Steven stresses the importance of faith in God and the eternal value of living a life of prayer and holiness. His heart is to see the lost saved and the Church strengthened.

Brother Steven stands by grace in the ministry office of the modern-day apostle. As a *sent one*, he is constantly traveling far and wide, throughout America and to the most remote areas of the world preaching the good news of Jesus Christ. Whether it is in the foothills of the Appalachian Mountains in his home state of North Carolina, or in the Himalayan Mountain region, or along the Nile River in Africa, Brother Steven has a mandate from God to *"Go, and teach all nations."* The outreach of his ministry includes television, internet, the printed page, crusades, revival meetings, and every other available means of sharing God's Word.

The television show *Fire and Glory* is rapidly growing with Steven's program now airing in over 30 nations with a potential viewing audience approaching two billion people. His books continue to expand in readership while igniting a desire within the reader for a more intimate walk with God. His first book, *Working With Angels*, is available in thousands of bookstores and is considered by many church leaders to be a timeless teaching on the subject of angels. His second book, *Standing on the Shoulders of Giants*, is a fascinating spiritual adventure that addresses the subject of biblical mantles. Steven offers keen insight and answers the questions that have intrigued and captivated the hearts of many modern saints, as well as those throughout church history.

Steven and his wife, Kelly, live in the western mountains of North Carolina and have two adult children, Matthew and Jennifer, along with their youngest daughter, Abigail. The ministry offices of Steven Brooks International are located in the historic downtown district of North Wilkesboro, North Carolina.

For booking information and upcoming meetings,
please visit our Web site at
www.stevenbrooks.org,
or e-mail us at
info@stevenbrooks.org.

Additional copies of this book and other
book titles from DESTINY IMAGE are
available at your local bookstore.

Call toll-free: 1-800-722-6774.

Send a request for a catalog to:

Destiny Image® Publishers, Inc.

P.O. Box 310
Shippensburg, PA 17257-0310

*"Speaking to the Purposes of God for This
Generation and for the Generations to Come."*

For a complete list of our titles,
visit us at www.destinyimage.com.